The Parson and the
Victorian Parish

The Parson and the Victorian Parish

by

PETER C. HAMMOND

HODDER AND STOUGHTON

LONDON SYDNEY AUCKLAND TORONTO

TO MY WIFE

Contents

Acknowledgments

The author wishes to thank the Oxford University Press for permission to use in this book material from *Lark Rise to Candleford*, published by the Oxford University Press and Penguin Books; the Estate of Mr. F. R. Fletcher and Jonathan Cape Limited, for permission to use material from *Kilvert's Diary*, edited by William Plomer; the Kingsmead Press for permission to use material from *The Journal of a Somerset Rector* by John Skinner, edited by Howard and Peter Coombs; the author and Hodder and Stoughton for material from *Armstrong's Norfolk Diary* by B. J. Armstrong.

Preface

FROM THE VESTRY walls they stare, tinted in sepia, with whiskers and beards, sitting in Glastonbury chairs, framed in passe-partout. They are the previous incumbents of the church, now long dead, who once ministered there and are now unregarded save for a casual glance, for little is known of them but their names and the years that they were in the parish. Now the present vicar prepares to take a service, while the churchwardens, perhaps, discuss the drains and the organist appears with a query on the psalm and the treasurer waves a bill that he finds inexplicable. The past vicars stare on, and the present one, catching sight of them, wonders what they were like, what were their hopes and fears, their failures and their achievements; and, sadly, acknowledges to himself that he will never know, for only a few fragments of their lives have they left behind them. Yet those few fragments are worth recording and this book attempts to sketch the work, the attitudes, the lives, of those who had the charge of parishes a hundred years or so ago.

The Established Church in England and Wales, and in Ireland, too, until 1871 when that Church was disestablished, was an ancient, complex, large, cumbersome organisation, and at the parochial level it creaked and groaned, yet somehow went forward in spite of its deficiencies, which were many. The clergy who had the charge of parishes, occupied positions of varying states, and a luxuriant nomenclature indicated the subtle gradations of this ecclesiastical scene. There were rectors who received and enjoyed all the tithes of a parish, being a tenth of the produce of its land. But in many parishes the tithes had been appropriated and were paid into the hand of persons, lay or ecclesiastical, who did not have the direct spiritual charge of the parishioners, in which case there was usually a vicar. It was realised, however, that even a vicar must live, so in these cases he most probably received the small tithes, which were the tithes on the minor produce of the land, such as lambs and chickens. By the nineteenth century the distinction between rectors and vicars meant little, for there were some vicars, like the vicar of Leeds, who were indubitably more important than some rectors; but the terms remained, and remain still, a survival from the past describing now a non-existent difference. Besides rectors and vicars there were ecclesiastical beings known as perpetual curates who, after 1838, were allowed to have the charge of parishes on somewhat different terms; and there were curates, too, who were virtually incumbents since the true incumbents of the parishes in which they worked were non-resident, or senile, or sick, or mad, or took no interest in parochial affairs. Nor should we omit the clergymen who had the charge of proprietary chapels, which were churches outside the parochial organisation of the Church, but which were influential in some places. The clergy who served in them ministered to discriminating congregations who paid rent for their pews and, though such clergymen might not be able to do all that a vicar did, yet they could exercise a considerable pastoral ministry among their flocks.

So, in the nineteenth century, the parochial clergy held their positions in a variety of ways and in consequence the terminology that describes this variety is plentiful. But we may call them all parsons. I use that term to describe any clergyman deeply involved at the parochial level in the work of the Church, though more particularly for those in charge of a parish.

The system within which these clergymen worked was astonishingly disorganised and illogical. For example, it might seem desirable that the right man should go to the right parish and that he should move from one parish to another if circumstances made that advisable. To achieve this some central authority, which had the power of appointing the incumbents and of moving them, would be required; but no such authority existed. The bishops did not possess it, for many others had the right of appointing parsons to livings besides themselves; nor could the bishops make incumbents move for, once appointed, they enjoyed the parson's freehold and could not be removed except for the most flagrant cases of heresy or immorality.

Yet the system gave a valuable independence to the parish priest and it produced great men; or perhaps it would be more true to say that it allowed great men to work in parishes. Dean Church observed, towards the end of his great history of the Oxford Movement, 'The English Church was after all as well worth living in and fighting for as any other; it was not only in England that light and dark, in teaching and in life, were largely intermingled and the mixture had to be largely allowed for.' The judgment is just.

To generalise is dangerous, so various were the forces and influences at work in the Victorian parish, but if we dare to generalise we might say that until the 1870s there was the feeling that the parochial clergy were better, more diligent, more numerous than those of the century before. They looked back and were conscious that they had higher standards than most of their Hanoverian predecessors. But after the 1870s the confidence that they possessed began to ebb. Doubt seemed, like a fog, to seep everywhere; the problem of evangelising the multitudes of the great cities began to appear to be insoluble; and the economic status of the clergy began to fall. The change was slow and not evident to everyone at the time; but, looking back, we can see Anglican incumbents rise in their position, and then fall a little, in the course of Victoria's reign.

I am most grateful to the Rev. Dr. V. H. H. Green, of Lincoln College, Oxford, for reading the typescript and for making suggestions for its emendation. To the staff of the Library at Sion College, London; St. Augustine's College, Canterbury; Canterbury Cathedral Library, and Deal Public Library I am also indebted and am glad to acknowledge their courtesy and their help. Finally, I owe a great debt of gratitude to my wife, who encouraged me in this project and did all the typing. Without her, the ideas in these pages would have remained only in my mind.

THE VICARAGE,
WALMER,
KENT,
JANUARY 1977

CHAPTER 1

The Patron

VICARS AND RECTORS died sometimes, and moved or were preferred sometimes, and resigned sometimes, though not very
frequently in the nineteenth century; and an army of patrons,
individual and corporate, lay and ecclesiastical, stood ready
to appoint to the vacancies so created. The system was complex, something of a gamble as Sydney Smith pointed out, and
involved the participation of a considerable body of people. A
clergyman desiring a living had to search for a patron willing
to present him to the living in his gift and then to wait for that
living to become vacant. Some found this supremely easy.
Others found it difficult indeed.

At the head of this army of patrons there was the Crown
which, on the advice of the Prime Minister of the day, selected
vicars and rectors for certain parishes scattered up and down
the land. The Crown appointed the vicars of Halifax. It chose
rectors, too, for the parish of St. Margaret, Westminster, and
sharp words passed between the Queen and Viscount
Palmerston in 1864 over the appointment there when Palmerston had submitted the name of one clergyman only to the
Queen, at which the Queen was not amused and told her
Prime Minister so, since it deprived her of any choice in the
matter. But a Prime Minister who believed that it was right to
use firm and stout language to the French Government and to
Frenchmen and had ordered a blockade of the Greek coast
without consulting his allies, was not the man to let the

Queen's protest go unchallenged. He replied to Her Majesty, therefore, pointing out that he was her responsible adviser in such matters, hinting that she must have other and irresponsible advisers, but so far submitting as to forward two names for her consideration. Still the Queen was displeased. 'The Queen,' she answered, 'makes it a rule, as the Prince did, to make enquiries in various quarters . . .'[1] The Queen and her various prime ministers engaged in a form of dialectic over ecclesiastical appointments that were not confined to the higher reaches of the Church, for the Crown had livings in its gift.

The Crown had also another finger in the parochial pie. If it took an incumbent from a living and made him a bishop or a dean it claimed the right of appointment to the vacated living, setting aside for that purpose the rights of the usual patron of the parish. In the months before Victoria's accession the vicar of St. Peter's-in-the-East at Oxford was chosen for the bishopric of Salisbury. The Crown, therefore, must appoint his successor at St. Peter's and the parishioners petitioned, as they sometimes did and do, that their curate might be allowed to fill his place. Lord Melbourne was Prime Minister and Lord Melbourne hesitated, remembering no doubt the storm that had raged in Oxford the year before when he had appointed Dr. Hampden as Regius Professor of Divinity, who was known to be friendly to dissenters and whose orthodoxy was suspect. 'Oxford is a conspicuous place,' Melbourne ruefully observed, 'the University stands in a particular situation with respect to the King's government, a small appointment there may have a great effect; and in such a matter a minister is not left at liberty to indulge his own feelings and inclinations.' But the curate proved after all to be acceptable and was appointed vicar. No storm this time ensued and in due course he, too, was promoted to the bishopric of Salisbury.[2]

The other minister of state who by reason of his office found himself deeply involved in parochial patronage was the Lord Chancellor. He appointed, for example, the vicars of Tewkesbury. It was a Whig chancellor, Lord Cottenham, who in 1847 presented the Rev. George Gorham to the living of

Brampford Speke, near Exeter, which led to one of the most celebrated cases of ecclesiastical litigation in the nineteenth century. The bishop, Phillpotts of Exeter, fiery Tory and high Churchman, disapproved of Mr. Gorham and in particular of his views on baptism which to the bishop seemed at variance with the teaching of the baptismal services set out in the Prayer Book of the Church. The bishop, therefore, declined to admit Mr. Gorham to the living. Gorham took the case to court and after many months of learned argument was victorious. The bishop threatened to excommunicate any who should institute and induct Mr. Gorham to Brampford Speke but, nevertheless, in August 1850 he was admitted to the living by commission and in September preached his first sermon there to a large and curious congregation. The Lord Chancellor had had his way but as a result Henry Wilberforce seceded to the Church of Rome and Manning edged nearer in that direction.

Henry Wilberforce, son of the great William Wilberforce, and brother of Samuel Wilberforce who was to be a notable bishop, first of Oxford and then of Winchester, had, like Mr. Gorham, benefited from the patronage of the Lord Chancellor. Seven years before he joined the Church of Rome he had been the vicar of Walmer, a poor living in Kent, from which he found it desirable to move to something richer. His brother Samuel, not yet a bishop, was Archdeacon of Surrey and more significantly, chaplain to Prince Albert, able, therefore, to whisper to the right people in the corridors of power. In 1843 it became known that Mr. Lutwidge, the vicar of East Farleigh near Maidstone, was dying and the living of East Farleigh with its comfortable stipend was in the gift of the Lord Chancellor. Samuel Wilberforce lost no time in mentioning to his great friend Mr. Anson, secretary to Prince Albert, that if the living should fall vacant his brother might be just the person to take it. Mr. Anson spoke to the Prince. The Prince wrote at once to Lord Lyndhurst, the Lord Chancellor, desiring in the Queen's name and his own that the living might be bestowed upon Henry, for it was his and the Queen's greatest wish to gratify Archdeacon Wilberforce in this matter. Lord

Lyndhurst obliged and Henry Wilberforce was appointed.[3]

The Queen, her prime ministers and her lord chancellors held in their hands a fair slice of patronage at the parochial level in the Church. The Queen was immutable and always there but prime ministers and lord chancellors came and went according to the rise and fall of political fortune, defeated or victorious over matters that were far from ecclesiastical. Readers of *Barchester Towers* will recall how the death of the old and placid Bishop of Barchester, a few hours after the fall of a ministry, killed Archdeacon Grantly's hopes that he might step into his father's shoes. It was Dr. Proudie who became the bishop—and Mrs. Proudie, too. Trollope here was describing fictionally what was perfectly possible. A change of ministry meant a change of patronage and the prospects of aspiring vicars as of aspiring bishops might be affected by sudden changes in the political scene. Thus, in 1858, an Italian conspirator, Felice Orsini, attempted in France the assassination of Napoleon III and nearly succeeded. In the investigation that followed it was discovered that the plot had been hatched in London and the bombs obtained from Birmingham. Palmerston, therefore, attempted to tighten the laws of conspiracy but was defeated and resigned, to be replaced by the Earl of Derby and a new Cabinet, Earl Granville replacing Lord Cranworth as Lord Chancellor. Little Rissington with West Rissington in Gloucestershire, small parishes which with many others were in the Lord Chancellor's gift, woke up to find that they had a new patron. Such was the far-flung effect Orsini's plotting had.

Bishops and archbishops led the clerical regiment of patrons, sometimes appointing to livings far beyond their own diocesan or provincial boundaries as the Archbishop of Canterbury did when he chose vicars for Blackburn. They increased their patronage in the nineteenth century and a windfall came their way in 1840 when the Cathedrals Act, passed because cathedrals were unpopular and thought by many to be over-staffed, absurdly rich and largely useless, transferred the individual patronage of deans and canons to their bishops. The Dean of York, therefore, who had been accustomed to appoint the vicars of Pocklington, found himself deprived of this right which was transferred to his archbishop. Bishops, too, might on their own account endeavour to increase the number of livings in their gift and the energetic Wilberforce succeeded in increasing his episcopal patronage in Oxfordshire from nine livings to thirty-nine during his twenty-four years' tenure of the see.[4] St. Saviour's, Southwark, now Southwark Cathedral, had been purchased by the parishioners from Henry VIII and consequently had the right of electing their own clergy, paying them by an annually levied rate. In 1883 the parishioners were relieved of their rate, the Ecclesiastical Commissioners furnished an endowment for the newly created rector and his two curates, and the patronage of the living was transferred to the Bishop of Rochester.[5]

Bishops enjoyed appointing their relations to the rich livings in their gift and the early nineteenth century saw some spectacular examples of nepotism in this respect. Bishop Sparke of Ely enriched his two sons and his son-in-law with benefices worth in total twelve thousand pounds a year and it was said that you could find your way across the fens at night by following the 'little sparks' planted in the livings of the diocese. *The Black Book*, published in the 1820s and the 1830s by a journalist, John Wade, and immensely popular, fulminated against abuses both in Church and State and deplored the sorry fact that a large mass of ecclesiastical wealth was appropriated to the maintenance of an indolent and luxurious priesthood. Cardinals in Rome, he suggested, were less generously rewarded than the clergy of the Established Church. The wings of episcopal patronage were soon to be clipped, however, by the restriction on pluralities, which prevented the heaping of ecclesiastical preferment on a beloved son's head. Bishops did not cease to help their relations who were in holy orders, but they could not now be so generous as in the past, finding the law against them. They did what they could, however. Bishop Phillpott's eldest son was ordained priest in 1831 and within a fortnight of his ordination was offered by his father the vicarage of Uny Lelant with Towednack in west Cornwall. This was designed as a stepping-stone to something better, for the bishop wished his son to be Precentor of Exeter Cathedral, a scheme scotched by the Dean and Chapter of Exeter who did not relish another and a younger Phillpott coming among them. The resulting problem for the bishop was then neatly solved by transferring the vicar of Grimley in Worcestershire into the precentorship, thus permitting the bishop's son to move to Grimley where the living was worth twelve hundred pounds a year.[6] A clergyman who was not a bishop's son might find his way into a good living by marrying a bishop's sister or a bishop's daughter, coming by this means to bask in the warmth of episcopal beneficence. Bexhill was thought to be the richest living in the diocese of Chichester. When it became vacant in the 1830s, Bishop Maltby resolved that his brother-in-law should have it. Much later in the century Archbishop Thomson of York gave his brother-in-law several pieces of preferment, crowning them with the offer of the benefice of Stokesley which, like Grimley, was worth twelve hundred pounds per annum and, indeed, a little more.

Thomson of York and his brother bishops might also use their patronage to further their own brand of churchmanship, whatever that might be. The low church Thomson wanted low church vicars and when Thorold, a protégé of Thomson's, went to Rochester as bishop in 1877 he, too, liked his vicars to be low. The parish of St. Paul's, Lorrimore Square, London, at that time in the diocese of Rochester, had the bishop as its patron, a sick vicar and a considerable ritual in its church. The vicar, knowing that he might not much longer be able to continue in the living and not wanting a low church bishop to appoint his successor, for a successor appointed from that quarter would probably look askance at the elaborate worship at St. Paul's, exchanged benefices with a priest holding views similar to his own, seeking by this means to preserve the traditions of the parish. But it was the new vicar that died unexpectedly, so that the bishop after all was able to exercise his patronage and did so by appointing his chaplain to the living. The bishop and his chaplain were resolved to alter the churchmanship of the parish from high to low and the bishop ventured like a daring Daniel into the lion's den by going down to preach there to tell the people of his intentions. Like Daniel, too, he emerged unmarked from the experience, though protesters hissed him after the service, knocked off the hat of his coachman and broke one of his carriage windows. But Thorold had his way.[7]

Deans and chapters, as we have seen, clung successfully to their corporate patronage, using it sometimes as the bishops did on behalf of their friends and their relations. The Dean and Chapter of Windsor held the patronage of Wantage, Berkshire, and there the dean was also vicar, riding over to the parish twice a year, putting up at the Bear Inn to receive his tithes and returning home 'without leaving either his carpet bag or his blessing behind him'. The dean found useful the extra income of eight hundred a year which came to him from the living and a curate was left in charge between the visits to do a little work. But in 1846 the dean died, leaving deanery and benefice vacant behind him, and William Canning, Canon of Windsor, offered the parish of Wantage to his niece's husband. W. J. Butler, who was twenty-eight and curate of Dogmersfield in Hampshire. Butler accepted and so began a memorable ministry of thirty-four years which made Wantage renowned in the history of the church. In this case the exercise of patronage with a tinge of nepotism was wonderfully successful, though Butler would have been an exemplary priest in any parish that had the good fortune to receive him.[8]

Archdeacons and other clergy, by reason of their office, were patrons also. An ancient town might be conterminous with an ancient parish, possessing one vicar and one parish church. At Sheffield the parish contained the town and the surrounding countryside, with a population of a little over fourteen thousand in 1736; easily managed by one vicar if he had curates to assist him. But the furious rate of growth of these industrial centres in the nineteenth century meant that the single parish must be divided and new churches built if the

Church in any way was to be able to serve the people. New vicars therefore, were required and found; and since they exercised their ministry in territory that had once been part of the ancient parish of the town they were in many cases appointed by the vicar of the ancient parish and given the lesser status of perpetual curate. They did not possess the freehold of their benefices and could be removed from them by revocation of the licence of the bishop but could not be dismissed at the behest of the vicar who had appointed them. The vicar of Blackburn appointed to twenty-one perpetual curacies; the vicar of Halifax appointed to nineteen.

The patronage of more than half of the livings in the Church of England was in private hands, and in the countryside the proportion was higher still. The nobility and the landed gentry would inherit with their rolling acres the advowsons of the livings on their estates and these were as much part of their property as the farms and fields that they possessed. The complete squire, patron of the parish and resident in it, saw his wishes fulfilled both in his village through which he frequently passed, and in his village church were he was accustomed to worship Sunday by Sunday. An extreme example of such a relationship between patron and incumbent is, of course, in *Pride and Prejudice*, where Lady Catherine de Bourgh's every word is received as manna from heaven by Mr. Collins, her rector, who revolves like a planet round her sun. Not every incumbent was as obsequious as Mr. Collins but every incumbent had need to take account of the views of his squire and patron. There were anxious days at Langley Burrell in 1874 when the squire dismissed the chief singer in the church and the rector and his family installed an harmonium there to lead the singing. The reaction of the squire to this innovation was anticipated with foreboding and some violence of language from him was expected, but all went off well as the squire, who went to church twice on the Sunday after the harmonium had arrived, said nothing at all. Sometimes, though, squire-cum-patron and incumbent worked harmoniously together and then they made up a formidable team. William Heathcote had been John Keble's pupil at Oxford and when, unexpectedly, he succeeded to his uncle's baronetcy and estate at Hursley, five miles from Winchester, he did not rest until he had secured Keble for the living there. Heathcote refused to let his farms and cottages to dissenters, preferring to let to less skilful farmers or to leave the farms untenanted rather than to allow them to profit from his acres; and when Hursley Church was rebuilt in heavy-handed fashion in 1848 he gave the spire.[9]

Yet another part of the army of patrons was composed of corporate bodies, some lay, some clerical, some mixed and some, as the nineteenth century advanced, changing from one into the other. In 1835 municipal corporations had been reformed by Act of Parliament and, because it was feared that they might be flooded with dissenters, they were directed to sell the ecclesiastical patronage which was in their hands. So Liverpool and Bristol and Norwich lost their right to appoint certain vicars, along with Bath and Bedford and Boston and others, and the patronage was sold to wealthy men or to the party trusts which were springing up to further churchmanship of one kind or another. That stalwart evangelical, Charles Simeon, bought the advowson of Bath Abbey so that in future rectors of an evangelical complexion would be able to preach to its fashionable congregation; and it is owned by the Simeon Trustees to this day.[10]

The universities of Oxford and Cambridge and their constituent colleges each held a considerable patronage in their hands, which they used in favour of their members. Balliol College, Oxford, offered the college living of Huntspill in Somerset to William Lake, one of her fellows, in 1858 and Lake found it pleasant enough there, with its rich dairy farms, remarking of the parish, 'the more you handle the rose bush the more thorns you find, but the roses still keep their scent'. The universities at the beginning of Victoria's reign were exclusively Anglican and their governing bodies Anglican clergy, but as the reign progressed their complexion changed utterly. In 1854 dissenters were admitted for the first time to Oxford and in 1856 for the first time to Cambridge, while between 1856 and 1858 the colleges at Oxford began the task of modifying their ancient statutes and, in doing so, modified to some extent the obligation of the fellows to be in holy orders. In 1871 nearly all religious tests at universities were swept away and when Victoria died the patronage that they possessed was administered no longer by the clergy of the Established Church but by bodies of a very different complexion; Anglicans, who might be clerical or lay, dissenters, catholics and non-believers. They were not, however, deprived of their patronage in the Church of England and keep it even now.

The cogs and spindles of yet more machinery which was set in motion in some parishes when a vicar had to be appointed can be illustrated by three examples taken from different areas of the country, showing how intricate might be the processes that were involved.

Dr. Williamson, the headmaster of Westminster School, decided in 1836 to hold a dinner party and invited to it a barrister from Leeds, Mr. Robert Hall, and Mr. and Mrs. William Page Wood. Mr. Wood, having a feverish cold, could not attend but Mrs. Wood, somewhat reluctantly, decided that she ought to go. At dinner she sat next to Mr. Hall and told him of the great work that a friend of hers and of her husband was doing in the parish of Holy Trinity at Coventry; his name being Walter Farquhar Hook. Next year the vicar of Leeds died unexpectedly. The right of the appointment of the new incumbent was vested in twenty-five trustees, of whom Mr. Hall was one and his father another, his father being the senior trustee. Mr. Hall's mind was carried back to the conversation at the dinner table of the previous year and he decided to enquire further into the merits of this vicar from Coventry about whom he had heard such an excellent report. The enquiry confirmed Mrs. Wood's testimony and Hook seemed to be the man for Leeds. However, there were still difficulties ahead, for Hook refused to go to Leeds to preach a trial sermon and he was known to hold to high church principles. Certain of the trustees decided, therefore, to go to Coventry to see Hook and his parish, which they did, and, like the Queen of Sheba before King Solomon, were impressed by what they saw. Hook, with his large lips and red hair, was elected to the living of Leeds by sixteen out of the twenty-three trustees present at the meeting; a most successful choice, for he transformed the parish and showed how effectively in a large town the church could work.[11]

No one could pretend that Combpyne in Devon was as large as Leeds. It rejoiced, however, in having two patrons for the parish, of whom one was catholic. But by law no catholic could present to a living in the Church of England and should a catholic possess such patronage it was transferred, according to that part of the country it was in, to one or other of the ancient universities. It seemed to Bishop Phillpotts, therefore, that in this case half the patronage of Combpyne should be exercised by Oxford University, which should jointly with the other patron appoint a rector to the living. Mrs Edwards, the other patron, took another view; that in these circumstances she might act as sole patron, and so tendered an instrument of presentation without consulting Oxford. The bishop refused her choice and made his own selection for the parish, rousing the wrath of Mrs. Edwards who took the case to court and in the Court of Common Pleas defeated the pugnacious bishop.[12]

In the thirteenth century Baldwin of Parndon bequeathed his estates and the advowson of Great Parndon in Essex to his three daughters as co-heiresses; six hundred years later his action was still affecting the patronage of the parish which as a result of this bequest came to be shared among three patrons who in turn presented to the living. Naturally the patrons changed frequently in the course of time, but the rotation of the patronage continued as the centuries passed, a patron exercising his right of presentation and then resting from his labours until the two other patrons had each in their turn presented, before his turn came again. The Crown, at one time, became one of the patrons; and Edward VI gave this patronage to the City of London which, in its turn, bestowed it upon the three hospitals of Bridewell, St. Thomas's and Christ's. St. Thomas's Hospital secured the whole of this patronage in the end, though it remained only one of the three patrons of the living and had to take its turn with the two others that presented to the benefice. So it came about in 1858 that the governors of St. Thomas's Hospital appointed the new rector to Great Parndon but did not present to that living again till 1909 when they nominated a man who had once been assistant chaplain at the hospital, for two other patrons appointed two other rectors in the intervening years.[13]

Like God upon Mount Sinai handing down the tables of the law to an expectant people, so patrons handed down vicars to waiting parishioners who had no say in these appointments. But this is not wholly true. A few parishes were to be found, like Chapel-en-le-Frith, where resident freeholders possessed the patronage of the living; but it was more likely that a parish would make representations to the patron when there was a vacancy in the benefice, and sometimes the parishioners could be vehement indeed. At Haworth the patronage was vested in freeholders and trustees, subject to the approval of the vicar of Bradford who was the titular vicar of the area. Unwisely, the vicar attempted to introduce Patrick Brontë's predecessor into the living without reference to the parish and the parish rose in revolt. The new parson on his first Sunday in the parish saw his congregation leave the church with a clattering and clumping of clogs while he was reading the second lesson; on the second Sunday a man rode round the aisles during service time upon an ass, facing its tail and with as many old hats upon his head as he could carry; on the third Sunday the parish introduced a drunken chimney-sweep into the place below the reading-desk, from which he climbed clumsily up the pulpit steps to embrace the unfortunate Mr. Redhead; on the fourth Sunday Mr. Redhead was not there, having left the parish. The people bore him no grudge and when he returned to preach years later the parishioners showed him no ill-will; but they insisted on their rights.[14]

Kingsley at Eversley owed his possession of the benefice in part at least because of the pressure parishioners brought to bear upon Sir John Cope, patron of the living. The previous rector, John Toovey-Hawley, would, when slightly indisposed, send the clerk to church to announce that there would be no service there that day; he showed no general interest in the parish but had a particular interest in the female section of the congregation, so much so that the discovery of an indiscretion of 'a most revolting nature' with one of these ladies forced him to flee the country and to leave the living vacant. Kingsley had been curate at Eversley and diligent then in the discharge of his duties. The parish, therefore, petitioned Sir John that Kingsley be appointed rector, and Sir John agreed, so that in 1844 Eversley received this young man of twenty-five as its incumbent.[15]

If a clergyman was not well known to one of this multitude of patrons, he or his family, if they had money, might consider buying an advowson which gave the right of presentation to a benefice, for, like other property, advowsons could be bought and sold, the price depending primarily on the income of the living and the state, the size and situation of the parsonage, though other factors entered in as well. The vicar of Ashton-Hayes, near Chester, wrote indignantly to Palmerston in 1856 asking if the price of the advowson should be 'enhanced by the delicate health, or old age, of the present incumbent, by the local attractions of good society, beautiful country, and proximity to a first-class railway station'? The answer was in the affirmative, for all these matters affected the desirability of a parish and, therefore, the price paid to nominate its vicar. So there was a market for patronage, and though people objected to this buying and selling, public opinion in the nineteenth century was content to let it be. We find, then, relations of the clergy and the clergy themselves buying advowsons so that the clerical members of their families might be put into livings. Robert Landor, brother of the poet Walter Savage Landor, went as rector to Birlingham in Worcestershire in 1829 because his mother had purchased the advowson; and there in that secluded country parish he indulged his literary and artistic tastes, grew melons and kept in perfect order four acres of lawn before his house. The father of E. B. Ellman, a Sussex parson, bought the advowson of Berwick in Sussex in 1837 that his son might be put into the parish, though the son had never been there and had the strongest objection to such sales and purchases. However, this did not prevent him becoming rector of the parish in 1846, and continuing as such for sixty years. St. Alban's, Holborn, a remarkable anglo-catholic city parish, had one of the most famous curates in the Church of England in Father Stanton. His family being wealthy, his father bought the advowson of Tetbury in Gloucestershire, reputedly worth a thousand a year, thinking to place his son in the living when it fell vacant. Father Stanton never liked the transaction, never accepted the living, refused the bequest of the advowson when his father died and continued at St. Alban's where he declined a stipend, though for technical reasons it was found necessary to pay him annually five shillings.

It was possible not only to buy and sell advowsons, which gave the right of presentation to the owner in perpetuity, but to buy and sell the next presentation to a living, or the next two or three presentations. This was useless to a clergyman who wanted to present himself, since in Queen Anne's reign it had been made illegal, though there were ways and means of circumventing the prohibition in the Act. The problems that might arise in this area of the law could be knotty ones as the example of Great Coates shows. There Sir John Sutton, Bt., had a life-interest only in the advowson of the rectory but, being catholic, could not exercise his rights. He, therefore, sold his life-interest to a clergyman, a Mr. Walsh, who paid three thousand pounds for the right of presenting to this Lincolnshire living worth eight hundred a year, with house attached. The purchase, however, involved a risk, for should Sir John happen to die before the rector, then Mr. Walsh would get nothing since he had purchased the life-interest only; but, surveying the health both of Sir John and of the rector, he thought it likely that the rector would predecease Sir John, allowing him to make a presentation to the living, and he might even, if Sir John lived long, secure two presentations. In the event Mr. Walsh was fortunate to get one, for the rector died on May 30th, 1873 followed by Sir John six days later, and Mr. Walsh, by the fortunate order of the deaths, was able to present. So far nothing had occurred to cause the raising of a bishop's eyebrows, and no argument would have arisen if Mr. Walsh had then presented a friend or a relation to the benefice. But he resolved to present himself, at which the bishop, Christopher Wordsworth of Lincoln, thinking that this contravened the statute of Queen Anne which forbade the clergy to purchase next presentations and then to present themselves, refused him institution. Thereupon Mr. Walsh took the case to court and won, for the Court of Common Pleas decided that since Sir John had not sold the next presentation to the living, but only an uncertain interest in the advowson which might or might not give rights of presentation, he was entitled to the benefice. The bishop had to pay costs and, as damages, half-a-year's value of the living. The Archbishop of Canterbury through his vicar general instituted the fortunate Mr. Walsh to Great Coates.[16]

The Bishop of Lincoln in his palace at Riseholme was not alone in his feelings of discomfort at the activities of Mr. Walsh and others like him, and as the Queen grew old it seemed more and more unsatisfactory that a wealthy clergyman who might be a lazy priest, could buy patronage that would permit him to occupy a benefice; while a poor clergyman who might be excellent could not do this. In the army the sale of commissions had been abolished in 1871 after the startling superiority of the German Army had been demonstrated for all to see at Metz and at Sedan, proving that effective forces required officers to be efficient rather than to be rich, thus making it seem reasonable to suppose that the abolition of the sale of patronage might likewise be of advantage to the Church. But though a Conservative government nibbled at this problem in 1898, restricting the sale by auction of some patronage and making some other reforms, the sale of advowsons continued well into the twentieth century, for the whole system had its supporters. Canon Newbolt of St. Paul's told intending ordinands at Cambridge in 1901 that God was in the long run the only patron and that no man was moved from parish to parish without being the man that God wanted to be moved, a doctrine of infallible patronage called in to douse the flames of clerical discontent. The whole army of patrons, therefore, marched on and livings continued to be filled by the many and various individuals and groups who held patronage in their hands. Happy the clergyman who had a patron; without one no living was to be had. Yet it was odd that the vicars choral of York appointed the vicars of Nether Wallop in Hampshire and men wondered why it should be so.

NOTES

1   Owen Chadwick, *The Victorian Church*, Part ii, p. 330.
2   H. P. Liddon, *Walter Kerr Hamilton*, pp. 8, 9.
3   A. R. Ashwell, *Life of Samuel Wilberforce*, Vol. 1, p. 222.
4   Diana McClatchey, *Oxfordshire Clergy 1777–1869*, p. 10.
5   C. H. Simpkinson, *Bishop Thorold*, pp. 280–1.
6   G. C. B. Davies, *Henry Phillpotts*, pp. 115, 143.
7   C. H. Simpkinson, *Bishop Thorold*, pp. 126–128.
8   A. J. Butler, *Life & Letters of William John Butler*, pp. 36; 56.
9   Georgina Battiscombe, *John Keble*, p. 52, 81, 167, 174, 294.
10 Owen Chadwick, *op. cit.*, Part i, pp. 108–10.
11 W. R. W. Stephens, *Life and Letters of Walter Farquhar Hook*, pp. 193–207.
12 G. C. B. Davies, *op. cit.*, p. 219.
13 John L. Fisher, *The Deanery of Harlow*, pp. 147–61.
14 Mrs. Gaskell, *The Life of Charlotte Brontë* (Everyman Edition), pp. 18–19.
15 Susan Chitty, *The Beast and the Monk*, pp. 89–94.
16 J. H. Overton and Elizabeth Wordsworth, *Christopher Wordsworth*, pp. 250–3.

CHAPTER 2

Income

THE NEW VICAR or rector, having been presented by the patron to the living, now took possession of it, installed himself in vicarage or rectory or in the house that he had bought or rented in the parish, and surveyed the scene. Now he could begin to receive the stipend due to him as the incumbent, which would come to him most probably from a variety of sources of which he would already have informed himself. He would know now what was due to him, though the collection of his income might prove more difficult than he had first perceived.

It was probable that some of his stipend would come from tithe. In the distant past, before ever William the Conqueror had invaded England, men had been paying tithe so that priests might pray and offer up the Mass for souls living and departed; and in the countryside especially tithe was one of the facts of life, as inevitable as the rising of the sun or the cold days of Christmas, paid in the nineteenth century as in the centuries before to vicar or rector òr even to laymen who had got their hands on some of it, so that the ministry of the Church might be sustained. It was the rector who collected the tithes on the major crops, the greater tithes, while the vicar collected the tithes on minor produce. Some land was exempt from tithe altogether. There were anomalies.

Until 1836, unless farmer and parson had agreed upon a money payment in place of payment in kind, the incumbent was paid literally a tenth of the produce of the land. At the time of harvest he and the farmer would set out for the fields where a tenth of the harvest would be set aside, an operation which could cause much ill-will, suspicion and even blows. In 1822 the rector of Camerton in Somerset was given sixteen lambs as tithe and found that the sixteenth had a broken back; 'shabby manoeuvering' he described it in his diary. Two years later, in September 1824, he and a farmer looked out over a field of barley from which tithe was claimed. Tempers ran high and the argument hot and the rector gave the farmer a bloody nose.[1] Tithe was a source of friction and difficult to collect, especially where there was a multiplicity of tithe-payers, so that incumbents rarely managed to gather in all that was due to them. On tithe day in 1816 the rector of Wath, near Ripon, found his arrears of tithe to be fifty-nine pounds and was well satisfied.

Tithe paid in kind made for trouble in the countryside so that its commutation into money payments was welcome reform when it came in the Tithe Commutation Act of 1836. Now the clergy would no longer have to gather in their tenth of the produce of the farm at harvest time but could sit comfortably at home and in January read the *London Gazette* which gave them the corn controller's official statement of the respective average value of wheat, barley and oats over the previous seven years, upon which in future the payment of tithe was based. The Act, therefore, helped the clergy but it was not wholly helpful since it ordered also that no tithe was to be paid on improvements to the land after it was passed. When in the 1840s, therefore, the invention of cheap machine-made cylindrical pipes for the drainage of land improved production, and the introduction of the mangel-wurzel in the middle of the nineteenth century improved the range of cattle fodder that was available, these enriched the farmer but not those who received the tithe. Furthermore, hops, fruit and market gardens were exempt from the provisions of the Act and continued to cause trouble when clergy endeavoured to collect tithes from them, a right not abolished until 1886.

People grumbled over the tithe, as people will when their pockets are depleted, but most were willing to pay it to the clergy when it was thought that they needed it; and even in Essex they paid it, where matters were worst. It was a different matter when tithe had to be paid to a layman or to an organisation that was not ecclesiastical. In one parish Guy's Hospital held the greater tithes, distrained on a particular farmer when he refused to pay and eventually collected what was due after a riotous auction, though in the same parish the vicar's tithes had been paid without question. In another there were over a thousand tithe-payers, many of whom were required to pay a mere two or three shillings a piece, which would have been impossible to collect without the goodwill of the payers. In all, it was estimated in 1887 that the total tithe-rent charge was in the order of four million pounds a year, of which two-fifths was in the hands of laymen. The parochial ministry depended much on tithe.

Glebe was the land belonging to a benefice, which might be farmed by the incumbent himself if he saw fit, or let out to others for the best rent that he could get if he was no farmer and his interests lay elsewhere. John Allen, Archdeacon of Salop, recalled how at the beginning of the nineteenth century his mother had farmed the glebe of the living of which his father was the rector and that she knew exactly how many furrows a man might plough in a fair day's work. The eccentric Hawker of Morwenstow on the North Cornish Coast himself farmed his seventy-two acre glebe, rented additional fields, refused to employ new techniques and machinery, but appears to have been shrewd and quite successful on the land. The amount of glebe held with a living was notoriously unequal. In Oxfordshire in 1869, eighty-four parochial clergy held more than thirty acres of it; forty-eight more than one hundred; fourteen more than three hundred, while two were well up in the landed gentry class with more than one thousand acres each. The amount varied also between county and county, for in the diocese of Rochester the average amount of glebe per benefice was five acres, but in the diocese of Peterborough it was one hundred and twenty-nine. Glebe could be much or little, scattered or compact, good soil or bad soil, pasture or arable. In the eighteenth century it had increased at the expense of tithe, for with the enclosures the chance was often taken of exchanging the tithe on the area to be enclosed for a new piece of glebe, an operation fairly performed it seems, with the clergy getting their fair share in the new arrangements. Glebe was, with tithe, the chief foundation of the income of the parochial clergy.

But the poor are always with us and there was no exception for the clergy, some of whom might find themselves in livings that were very poor indeed, without tithe or glebe, or with little of either. Two institutions of the Church, centrally administered, tried to help the poor Victorian parsons, Queen Anne's Bounty and the Ecclesiastical Commission; they did much good, but neither was able to solve the problem since they never commanded sufficient funds to do so. Queen Anne's Bounty, founded by that Queen who returned to the Church taxes that the Crown had received since the Reformation, could hardly afford to be bountiful on its income of fifteen thousand pounds a year. It relieved the poverty of the incumbents of small country livings with stipends under two hundred pounds per annum and many were grateful for its help; but though it resolved in 1824 to bring all benefices up to the value of fifty pounds a year, one of its speakers before a parliamentary committee in 1868 had perforce to admit that some livings still had an income that was less than this. The Bounty, too, made loans for parsonages at rates of three and a half to four per cent repayable over a period of thirty-one years though, sadly, it had to bring actions against incumbents that could not repay what they had borrowed. The Ecclesiastical Commission, offspring of the movement for reform in the 1830s, the child of the efficent Peel, grew to be more important than Queen Anne's Bounty. Begun in 1835, it was born out of the evident need to provide clergy for the mushroom growth of towns and cities and to pay them, for clergy in new benefices had no tithe, no glebe, since what there was remained with the parishes from which they had been carved. 'The mother parish ate the oysters: the districts divided the shells,' William Rogers of St. Thomas's, Aldersgate Street, London, complained. Money, therefore, was required and though many hoped wistfully that the State might help—had not the government as late as 1820 provided a hundred thousand pounds a year for the augmentation of poor livings?—no further golden eggs were forthcoming from that quarter. So men looked about, saw the rich indolence of numerous dignitaries attached to the cathedrals, noted poor priests labouring in vast parishes in great towns and observed that it might be possible to alter such a situation. Bishop Blomfield looked at London and said:

I traverse the streets of this crowded city with deep and sol-emn thoughts of the spiritual condition of its inhabitants. I pass the magnificent church which crowns the metropolis, and is consecrated to the noblest of objects, the glory of God, and I ask of myself in what degree it answers the object. I see there a dean, and three residentiaries, with incomes amounting in the aggregate to between £10,000 and £12,000 a year. I see, too, connected with the Cathedral, twenty-nine clergymen whose offices are all but sinecures, with an annual income of about £12,000 at the present moment, and likely to be very much larger after the lapse of a few years. I proceed a mile or two to the east and north-east and find myself in the midst of an immense population, in the most wretched state of destitution and neglect, artisans, mechanics, labourers, beggars, thieves, to the number of at least 300,000. I find there, upon an aver-age, about one church and one clergyman for every 8,000 or 10,000 souls; in some districts a much smaller amount of spiritual provision; in one parish, for instance, only one church and one clergyman for 40,000 people.[2]

The Cathedral Act of 1840, therefore, suppressed some three hundred and sixty non-resident prebends, some sine-cure rectories and some resident canonries, transferring their assets to the Ecclesiastical Commission, though nothing was to be done until death had removed prebendary and canon from the scene so that the money came in slowly in fits and starts. It took a long time for this harvest to be gathered, but in the 1880s eventually it was, as ancient dignitaries died and long leases on their estates at last fell in. In the early days, then, it was necessary for the Commission to move slowly, hampered by lack of funds and hampered, too, by bishops, all of whom were Commissioners, and some of whom demanded grand palaces, Bishop Longley of Ripon having fifteen thousand pounds of the Commissioners' money for his. By 1843 it was resolved to augment livings in public patronage with populations of two thousand or over to one hundred and fifty pounds per annum, and in 1864 it was hoped to raise within five years existing benefices in public patronage to three hundred pounds a year. By 1880 about four thousand seven hundred benefices had been augmented with six hundred and twenty thousand five hundred pounds in perpetuity, representing a capital sum of eighteen million six hundred and fifteen thousand pounds.[3]

Fees were paid to the clergy for certain services in the church, though in the country, where parishes were of small population, they barely affected the income of the incumbent since they were so few. In a parish where there might be, say, ten weddings a year and the payment for each, half-a-crown, it was not possible to grow rich on the fees of those who desired matrimony. The offerings made at the churching of women were also for the incumbent, the Prayer Book ordering that 'The Woman, that cometh to give her Thanks, must offer accustomed offerings'. Sabine Baring-Gould, author of 'Onward, Christian soldiers' and squire-cum-parson of Lew Trenchard on the edge of Dartmoor for forty-three years, once churched two girls who were unknown to him and when the clerk approached them with a pewter bowl for their offerings, a conversation interesting to the congregation ensued: 'Us b'aint mothers, nor us b'aint married.' 'Don't foller,' replied the clerk, and then: 'Why did you go into the Churching pew?' 'Us didn't know no better,' was the reply of the blushing girls. . . 'Then you ort,' said the clerk sententiously. 'But'—relaxing—'never you mind! Such pretty maids as you be, blushin' as rose-buds, you'll be sure before long to get 'usbands, and then you'll want to be churched. So you can give thanks afore that takes place.'[4] It was as well for Baring-Gould that he did not depend upon such offerings.

But in the towns it was different, for where there were parishes with huge populations the fees could be substantial. In 1838 the vicar of St. Giles-in-the-Fields, London, earned £174. 16s. 6d. from the burial of the dead and with the opening of Kensal Green Cemetary the vicar of Paddington lost fees worth two hundred pounds a year.[5] Where marriages and funerals took place in a parish daily, or almost daily, fees could mount up for its vicar in a very satisfactory manner. But the fees brought problems when a new church was built, for if marriages and funeral services were allowed in it and the fees for these services were paid to its incumbent, this meant that the vicar of the mother church, from whose parish the new parish had been taken, saw those fees taken from him also, which he was loath to see. In 1838 a generous donor built a church in Bradford, dedicated to St. James in the lancet Gothic style, and the Bishop of Ripon, Longley, licensed it for public worship. It had been agreed with the vicar of Bradford that the church might be used for those services for which fees could be charged and that those fees might become part of its new minister's stipend; but in 1839 there was a new vicar of Bradford who felt it not right to alienate the revenues of his benefice in this manner and revoked the agreement. The man who was to be the first incumbent of St. James, the 'ten hours parson', Parson Bull, famous for his support of the Factory Acts, was unwilling to take the post if he could not perform in the church all the services; so the donor, who had spent nearly fourteen thousand pounds on church, vicarage and school, kept the church in his own hands and closed it for two years.[6]

A church with pews to which are affixed thin brass frames of a size able to take a visiting card but now empty, is an indication that the vicar there was once able to increase his stipend by the letting of pews. The incumbent of the largest parish in Nottingham was entirely dependent on pew rents and the Easter Offering, though he was a pluralist and did well enough financially from other quarters. The ultimate examples of this form of paying for the preacher are to be found, however, not in parish churches but in proprietary chapels, owned by individuals or bodies of trustees and financed entirely by subscriptions and the rents that could be got from pews. The lease of Quebec Chapel in London had been purchased by J. H. Gurney, rector of St. Mary's, Bryanston Square, in whose parish the Chapel was situated, and to the Chapel went in 1853 Henry Alford, scholar of the New Testament in Greek and later Dean of Canterbury, who preached on Sunday mornings and afternoons to influential congregations composed of Members of Parliament, barristers and others prominent in London life. In return he received a stipend of four hundred pounds a year. Down in Brighton the father of Henry Venn Elliott bought the partly-finished chapel of St. Mary, completed it and left it to his son as part of his inheritance after his death. The Bishop of Chichester consecrated it in 1827 and there the son ministered until he died in 1865, founding an establishment where the daughters of poor clergymen could be trained as governesses for the higher and middle classes. He drove to church on Sundays claiming the right to do so under the plea of necessity, did not say grace after meals since it was not recorded in the Scriptures that the Saviour ever did so, and had the pew-openers wait after Sunday evening service till he came from the vestry, that he might shake hands with them and bid them good-night.[7]

Before the accession of Victoria some incumbents were paid by means of a church rate. At St. Botolph, Bishopsgate, the tithe would have brought in an immense sum if it could have been enforced; but it could not be enforced and Blomfield, then the rector there, secured a compromise whereby an income of two thousand pounds a year was to be raised for the living by a rate. At Holy Trinity, Coventry, where Hook was vicar before going on to Leeds, the income of the living likewise depended on a rate but as Hook never pushed against defaulters he seldom received more than half of the eight hundred pounds which he was entitled to expect. Church rates, however, were opposed by dissenters, voted down in annual vestry meetings amidst scenes of turmoil and wild confusion, and at length fell into desuetude. A parish, then, wishing to help its vicar who was poorly paid and yet had obligations, perhaps, to keep a curate or curates who were a charge on his own stipend, must do so voluntarily. At Greenwich a Church Council circular of 1888 reported that the total receipts of the living there were five hundred and one pounds a year, that stipends to curates and payments to lay agents amounted to four hundred and seventy pounds leaving the vicar thirty-one pounds; but there were also necessary subscriptions and the upkeep of a daughter church which turned this into a deficit. A Vicar's Fund was started which brought in on an average four hundred pounds a year, allowing the vicar, Brooke Lambert, to continue in the parish where he advocated cremation and freemasonry and surrounded himself with rare china, glass, furniture and prints. Other parishes gave a collection, usually at Easter, to their vicar. In 1873 Walsham How, prolific and popular hymn writer in the Victorian Church, was offered All Saints, Margaret Street, where the endowment brought in one hundred and fifty pounds a year and the vicarage was in the hands of curates; but it was supposed that the income was considerably increased by the custom of giving the offertory on one Sunday in the year, uncounted, to the incumbent. The Bishop of London did not know what it was worth. Towards the end of the century the use of the Easter Offering as a gift to the parson spread rapidly and by 1905 nearly half the parishes were said to use it in this way; by then parsons were poorer and parishes saw that they needed help.

The taking in of boarding pupils was a cottage industry that some of the clergy found to be profitable. For a year or so, between school and university, it was common practice for a young man who had parents with money to reside in a vicarage and polish up his classics and mathematics with a learned vicar before going up to Oxford or to Cambridge. Henry Alford, while a country parson, took in not less than sixty pupils in this way, boarding four or six at a time, and found later that three of them were in the House of Lords and five or six of them in the House of Commons. He started work with his pupils at ten a.m. and raised money for the restoration of the church at Wymeswold from their fees. A well-connected vicar who had been a fellow at a university might command two or three hundred pounds a year from each pupil so that, taking in six of them, he could increase his income by a thousand pounds or more. Other members of an incumbent's family might also take in pupils or attempt to do so. The Miss Brontës sketched out a prospectus for a school to educate a limited number of young ladies at the Parsonage, Haworth, and intended to charge thirty-five pounds a year for 'Board and Education, including Writing, Arithmetic, History, Grammar, Geography and Needle Work' with French, German, Latin, Music and Drawing at a guinea a quarter. The use of the pianoforte was extra and each young lady was to be provided with one pair of sheets, pillow cases, four towels and a dessert and tea spoon. Nothing came of the project; no young ladies appeared and Miss Branwell, the aunt, would not pay for the alterations to the house that would have been required.[8] Nevertheless, there were numerous little schools of boarding pupils scattered in vicarages up and down the land, though they decreased towards the end of the century as education became more technical and complex.

Macaulay, describing the parochial clergy in 1685, had this to say of them:

Hardly one living in fifty enabled the incumbent to bring up a family comfortably. As children multiplied and grew, the household of the priest became more and more beggarly. Holes appeared more and more plainly in the thatch of his parsonage and in his single cassock. Often it was only by toiling on his glebe, by feeding swine, and by loading dungcarts, that he could obtain daily bread; nor did his utmost exertions always prevent the bailiffs from taking his Concordance and his inkstand in execution. It was a white day on which he was admitted into the kitchen of a great house, and regaled by the servants with cold meat and ale.

His children were brought up like the children of the neighbouring peasantry. His boys followed the plough; and his girls went out to service.

But in the next century some of the clergy climbed several rungs up the social ladder, partly because in certain circumstances it was possible for one clergyman to amass a collection of livings in his own hands, to pay curates miserable stipends to do the duty in them, and to keep most of the income from them for himself, and partly because agriculture advanced and tithe and glebe increased in value. Not all incumbents were in a position to rise in this manner and many found themselves still at the bottom of the ladder, with the gap steadily widening between themselves and their more affluent and socially respectable brethren up above. Yet, speaking generally, there was an improvement in income and status, and the prosperity of the parson in the nineteenth century was founded on this progess in the eighteenth, on Lord Townsend's discovery of the value of turnips planted on a large scale, on Jethro Tull's improved system of sowing, on enclosures, on the introduction of the swede, kale, early clover and vetches, on the better rotation of crops, on the improved management of the land using clay marl to bind light soils together and chalk and lime to break down heavier ones, and on manure; so that by the time we come to Jane Austen we find that the cook at the parsonage is paid the same as the cook at Mansfield Park and that at Edmund's living of Thornton Lacey the farmyard must be removed from the proximity of its parsonage, which can be given the air of a gentleman's residence without any very heavy expense.

Many livings in Victoria's reign provided a comfortable income for their incumbents but there were wide variations in what they were worth. Doddington in the fens was among the wealthiest of them, where a stipend of eight thousand pounds a year was derived from land that had been reclaimed and went to an incumbent who would have been more at home in regency Bath, giving him more than most bishops received; while at Stanhope the rector had more than three thousand a year from the ore raised in the lead mines belonging to the bishopric of Durham. At the other end of the scale there were livings worth nothing, occupied by 'consecrated beggars' as Sydney Smith called them. In 1831 the parish of Cholesbury, near Tring, had a population of less than one hundred and fifty composed almost exclusively of paupers. The rates for all purposes were thirty shillings in the pound and in consequence all but eight acres were forced out of cultivation. The gates of the farms were taken down and fences left unrepaired in order that the owners might not be rated; the vicar made no attempt to collect his tithe since the rates on it far exceeded its value, and the glebe was useless, so that the incumbent was almost starved out of the living. In this case the provision of allotments transformed the situation, reduced the number of the poor and so the poor rate, and ten years later all was well.[9] The wide variation of income among the parochial clergy is nicely reflected in *Middlemarch* where George Eliot gives us portraits of Edward Casaubon, rector of Howick, living in a considerable mansion with much land attached to it while the curate occupies the parsonage; and Mrs. Cadwallader, wife of a poor rector, who was obliged to get her coals by stratagem and to pray to heaven for her salad oil.

Agricultural prices remained amazingly stable for forty years after the Queen came to the throne so that a living which had tithes of one hundred pounds in 1835 continued to receive about that amount for a long time; in such a parish the value of the tithe fell to £89. 15s 9d. in 1855 and rose to £112. 15s. 7d. twenty years later, remaining, therefore, substantially unchanged, so even were the prices of wheat and oats and barley. Even the repeal of the corn laws, so important politically, caused barely a tremor in the agricultural scene and the clergy continued to enjoy their share of the prosperity of the countryside. But across the Atlantic there were changes which would shake the foundations of British farming and with it the way of life of the parochial clergy; for the prairies were pouring grain into the trucks of the new railroads which moved it to the eastern seaboard where it was loaded into steamships for the passage over the sea. Aggravated by the shortage of gold, the price of grain fell in Britain and the price of land, too; and with the price of land fell the value of tithe and glebe from 1878 onwards, so that by 1901 the tithe of a parish that had been worth one hundred pounds in 1835 was down to £66.10s. 9d. The clergy noticed that they were growing poorer.

They did not, however, grow poorer at the same rate. Those whose income came from glebe suffered the most, for no one now wanted it or, if they did, they were prepared to pay for it only a paltry rent. In the Midlands, where land had once been let at forty or fifty shillings an acre, it fetched in 1887 perhaps ten or fifteen shillings an acre, for the heavy clay soils of Nottinghamshire, Northamptonshire and Lincolnshire had become unprofitable. On the other hand, those whose glebe was rich pasture suffered little or not at all, for milk and cream and butter, being perishable had to be produced near at hand. Pasture, therefore, continued to be in demand so that the clergy in those parts where dairy farming was the occupation of the countryside received almost as much as they had received in more prosperous times.

In a more leisurely age the clergy had not retired. Archbishop Vernon Harcourt of York died in his ninety-second year, soon after a wooden bridge had collapsed and thrown him and his chaplain into the pool below, at which he said to his chaplain, 'Well, Dixon, I think we've frightened the frogs.' The year was 1847 and for many years after bishops and incumbents continued in their dioceses and parishes until they sank into senility and expired, since there was no means of providing a pension for them. The Incumbents' Resignation Acts of 1871 and 1887 attempted to meet this problem for the beneficed clergy by arranging for the pension of the retiring incumbent to be paid out of the stipend of his successor, to the successor's direct loss and annoyance. It made life hard for a man who saw his income cut by as much as a third in order to pay his predecessor who, like Charles II, often appeared to be an unconscionable time in dying. A rector retired in 1877 from a living with glebe worth six hundred pounds a year and was given a pension of a third of that amount out of its stipend. Ten years later the value of the glebe had sunk to three hundred pounds per annum, leaving the present occupant of the benefice a mere one hundred pounds a year, for his predecessor still got his two hundred pounds. A comfortable living had become a poor one.[10]

It was fortunate that many of the clergy who had badly-endowed livings had well-endowed wives or private means themselves. Nevertheless, money was short in many vicarages and rectories where it had once been plentiful, as the Queen grew old. Richard Jefferies looked over the wall into the garden of one such parsonage somewhere in north Wiltshire or south Gloucestershire in the 1870s and noted the details with the keen eye of a reporter:

> Inside the enclosure the reverend gentleman himself reclines in an armchair of canework placed under the shade of the verandah, just without the glass door or window opening from the drawing-room upon the lawn. His head has fallen back and a little to one side, and an open book lies upon his knee; his soft felt hat is bent and crumpled; he has yielded to the heat and is slumbering. The blinds are partly down the window, but a glimpse can be obtained of a luxurious carpet, of tables in valuable woods and inlaid, of a fine piano, of china, and the thousand and one knick-knacks of highly civilised life. The reverend gentleman's suit of black, however, is not new; it is, on the contrary, decidedly rusty, and the sole of one of his boots, which is visible, is much worn.[11]

His wife, too, was there in the garden in a dress of the cheapest material, Jefferies noted, thinking of ways and means by which their income could be increased. She had tried goats, but no one liked their milk and they ate everything; then poultry, but they died of an epidemic; and after that market gardening, but the potatoes failed, the currant bushes were blighted, the strawberries were eaten by snails and there would be no asparagus for three years. She had tried painting illuminated texts but found that fifteen hours' hard work sold for threepence and the materials cost a shilling. Now she was pondering on the possible profitability of bees. But just as the legendary Dame Partington attempted in the middle of a storm, with mop in hand, to drive away the Atlantic Ocean from her door at Sidmouth, and found the contest to be unequal, so this lady found herself unable to defeat the economic forces ranged against her. The incomes of the clergy continued to slide and suggestions like those of Bishop Lightfoot that some well-endowed benefices could be reduced in value in order to improve others, or that all livings above a certain sum might be taxed for those that were poorer, fell on deaf ears. A bishop remarked to a reporter in 1887, 'we have uneven men, and we want uneven livings'. They remained uneven for a long time after that, until well into the twentieth century when tithe faded away, not without conflict; glebe continued a shadow of its former self; the Ecclesiastical Commissioners joined the Queen Anne's Bounty and as the Church Commissioners became the chief paymasters of incumbents; and parishes raised for the expenses of their vicar money that before had come unquestioned from his pocket.

NOTES

1   John Skinner, *Journal of a Somerset Rector*, pp. 198, 272–4.
2   S. C. Carpenter, *Church and People 1789–1889*, pp. 100–1.
3   G. F. A. Best, *Temporal Pillars*, pp. 214, 353, 447, 450 498.
4   S. Baring-Gould, *Early Reminiscences 1834–1864*, p. 147.
5   Owen Chadwick, *The Victorian Church*, Part I, p. 327.
6   J. C. Gill, *Parson Bull of Byerley*, pp. 128–31.
7   Josiah Bateman, *Henry Venn Elliott*, pp. 113, 116, 149, 270–1, 387.
8   Winifred Gerin, *Charlotte Brontë* pp. 273–5.
9   John Sandford, *Parochialia*, pp. 430–1.
10   Herbert P. Thomas, *The Church and the Land*, p. 87.
11   Richard Jefferies, *Hodge and his Masters*, Vol. I, p. 150.

CHAPTER 3

The Parsonage

IT WAS NOT obvious in the early years of the nineteenth century that the clergy need reside in their parishes. In a small living set in deep countryside it was thought sufficient for the parson or his curate to appear on a Saturday, perhaps take a look around the parish and visit any who needed visiting and on the Sunday take the morning service, in which might be included the occasional baptism, marry any who desired matrimony and church any that wanted churching, before going away again until the next Saturday came round. The occasional funeral might require his presence in the week, or the presence of some other clergyman living in the district, but no other duties seemed to be required of him so that he could do what he liked and live where he liked the rest of the time, leaving his parish to get on with its own affairs as it saw fit. In 1836 Campbell Tait, the future Archbishop of Canterbury, was licensed to the curacy of March Baldon and Toot Baldon, five miles from Oxford. The two churches were in bad repair and there was no vicarage for the vicar was resident abroad through ill-health, so that Tait, then a young fellow of Balliol, would ride over on a Saturday night to a hired cottage at the Baldons, take Sunday duty, and return to Balliol in time for the college service on Sunday afternoon. For many clergymen the countryside held no attractions; they preferred to reside in market towns near their benefices, enjoying congenial company, rather than live among their rude parishioners.

Lewes in Sussex was called the Rookery, from the number of clergy who rode out from there in black coats on Sundays to do duty, though not all managed even that, for the curate of Berwick in over six years never once saw his rector in the parish though he lived at Lewes a mere six miles away. Bishop Kaye of Lincoln noticed the same phenomenon at Louth and resolved to disturb that nest of rooks.

In parishes where the incumbent was non-resident it could hardly be expected that the parsonage would be more than modest, if one existed at all, which often it did not. Since the vicar of Wantage was the Dean of Windsor until 1846, the new vicar, W. J. Butler, when he arrived, found the vicarage had not been inhabited by the incumbent and thought it to be the coldest house that he had ever lived in, ancient, thatched, dilapidated, with thin walls through which snails found their way into the drawing-room. He built a new vicarage in 1850. In a return of 1835, one thousand seven hundred and twenty-eight parsonages were reported as unfit to live in, though we must regard this figure with suspicion since it was produced by incumbents who were seeking to justify non-residence; and two thousand eight hundred and seventy-eight livings had no parsonage at all. If a house existed and was occupied by a curate or used to accommodate a clergyman on a Saturday night due to take duty in the parish on Sunday morning, then there was no incentive to improve it or to repair it or to enlarge it and so it fell into decay.

The appearance of an incumbent or his curate in church on a Sunday and his disappearance before the day was over for the rest of the week from the parish in which he was supposed to exercise his ministry, did not appear to be the best way of fulfilling that ministry in the church; and the complete absence of a vicar who never came near his benefice and was totally invisible to his parishioners meant that such a clerical absentee could exercise no ministry at all. So a campaign was mounted to get the clergy into the parishes and to keep them there, a campaign that was successful though never competely so. In 1777 the opening shot in this battle was fired when Acts of Parliament, known as Gilbert's Acts, announced that 'many of the parochial clergy, for want of proper habitations, are induced to reside at a distance from their benefice, by which means the parishioners lose the advantage of their instruction and their hospitality', and made it possible for the clergy to obtain loans for parsonages. Two other Acts followed in 1803, making it more difficult for the clergy to be non-resident and catching up in a leisurely way some startled incumbents who found that they must reside in their parishes. Sydney Smith had been presented to the living of Foston-le-Clay in Yorkshire in 1806, but remained in the south for the next three years, visited the parish only once in that time, and appointed a neighbouring curate to take the duty. In 1808 Vernon Harcourt became Archbishop of York and the placid man began to demand residence of his clergy so that Sydney Smith found himself compelled to move to Yorkshire, though not into his parish, for he lived at Heslington, near York, driving over to Foston every Sunday, which was a dozen miles away. The parsonage at Foston was a hovel as there had been no resident incumbent since the days of Charles II, and the amiable archbishop did not demand that a new one should be built; but since it appeared probable to Sydney Smith that he would be immured there for the rest of his life he decided to build and to move into the parish. The new house cost over four thousand pounds, was ready for occupation in 1814, and was commodious and pleasant, even though the chimney-pieces had to be of Portland stone, not marble. Unusual features of this residence included air tubes which pierced the outer walls and opened into the centre of the grates, keeping the fire bright; a great speaking trumpet near the front door, through which he could shout directions to his labourers in the fields; and a telescope, with which he could keep them under observation. Sydney Smith was not a man to suffer in silence and complained, 'a diner-out, a wit, and a popular preacher, I was suddenly caught up by the Archbishop of York, and transported to my living in Yorkshire, where there had not been a resident clergyman for a hundred and fifty years. Fresh from London, not knowing a turnip from a carrot, I was compelled to farm three hundred acres, and without capital to build a parsonage house.' 'My living in Yorkshire,' he said, 'was so far out of the way that it was actually twelve miles from a lemon.'[1]

The clergy were more closely corralled in their cures by the Pluralities Act of 1838, which ordered that one person could not hold more than two benefices, that these benefices must be within ten statute miles of one another, that neither of them must have a population larger than three thousand, and that their joint value was not to exceed one thousand pounds. The plurality required dispensation from the Archbishop of Canterbury and the Act strengthened the powers exercised by the bishops in enforcing residence. In 1850 the restrictions were made more severe; livings must now be within three miles of each other and the annual value of one must not exceed one hundred pounds; while thirty-five years later the rules were relaxed a little and the twentieth century has seen a return to the situation which eighteenth-century incumbents knew well. But in Victorian times more clergy were resident in more parishes than ever before or since and there were more vicarages and rectories because there were more men available, more money to pay them and to house them and the conviction that they should reside was strong.

Some of these houses were very large, either having come down from an earlier age or having been extended or newly built in the nineteenth century. A mansion from earlier days, built as a rectory and inhabited as such until 1956, is at Hampton Lucy near Warwick. The Lucy family, which owned the estate and held the patronage of the living, built this classical, restrained, dignified, opulent house in 1721–2 for any of its members who might have a taste for the clerical profession and therefore money was lavished upon this sumptuous residence. In 1815 John Lucy installed his younger son, another John, as rector and there he remained till his death fifty-nine years later. Never an active parish priest in the proper sense of the word, but every inch a gentleman, 'he would sweep off his hat with punctilious politeness to an old woman picking up sticks: talked of a cowcumber and a balcōny, dined at two o'clock and rose at four, would not allow pork at his table or

persons holding Radical views inside his house'. He put the
fear of God into the children of the parish, gave out fox-
hunting notices from the pulpit, and when in 1874 he was not
expected to live he would drink a bottle and a half of cham-
pagne in twenty-four hours and a bottle of brandy in three
days. His Alderney cow was milked at one in the morning for
a cup of its milk with a spoonful of brandy in it and he rose
from his sick-bed to go to London to get a new set of teeth and
stayed six weeks, though his doctor said that the railway journey would kill him.[2]

Many parsonages built before the nineteenth century,
however, were not nearly so grand as that at Hampton Lucy
and were, the Victorian clergy thought, too small for their
needs and for their rank in life. They looked at these modest
dwellings and decided to improve and enlarge them, adding a
wing here or an extra storey there or extending the stables and
the servants' quarters so that their houses would meet their
requirements and proclaim the fact that they were gentlemen.
At Bemerton, near Salisbury, that great parish priest, George
Herbert, had built, in the seventeenth century, his own parsonage, a plain gabled building of flint with stone dressings
and mullion windows, which was greatly extended in the
nineteenth century to accommodate the rector and his wife,
four daughters, ten indoor servants, two gardeners and two
stablemen. One of the vicars of St. Mary Abbots, Kensington,
adopted the policy of 'another baby, another room', for lay
and clerical families alike grew larger, not because wives bore
more children but because more of them survived. In 1740
seventy-five out of every hundred children died at birth or
before they were six, while at the beginning of the nineteenth
century this had fallen to forty-one per cent. There were,
therefore, more mouths to feed and more people to sleep, so
that the large Victorian vicarage or rectory did not seem over-
large when there were a dozen children to be housed,
together with the numerous servants that were required to
run such an establishment. Enlargements, then, were commonplace, and even houses that had been erected early in
Victorian times received additions, like the rectory at Long

Melford, Suffolk, which was built then in Tudor style but was enlarged in 1878 into a rambling residence of five reception rooms, sixteen bedrooms and three dressing-rooms, a house fit to match the vast spaces of Long Melford's church.

If there were pupils as well to be taken in so that the parsonage was to serve also as an educational establishment, then a large house was obviously required. Creeton in Lincolnshire had a population of sixty-four and the rector a benefice worth one hundred and sixty-one pounds a year. He borrowed four hundred and seventeen pounds in 1851 for an extension to his rectory in order to accommodate his pupils. Another incumbent obtained a loan which paid for an additional room at the parsonage to be used for parish purposes, but which also served as a billiard-room for the recreation of his students. His successor found that he was obliged to repay what had been borrowed. Towards the end of the century such schemes began to be more closely scrutinised as clerical incomes shrank and parsonages remained apparently unshrinkable.[3]

A new house might be built if the old parsonage were dilapidated or inconvenient or badly placed or not to taste, and a new house might be needed also if there had been no parsonage before. Some of these Victorian vicarages and rectories were on an impressive scale, substantial ecclesiastical residences for vicars who were well-to-do and rectors who were wealthy. John Skinner of Camerton in Somerset rode over one day in 1821 to see the new parsonage being erected at Priston and noted that it appeared to be on a large scale. Clergy in his neighbourhood, he observed, were by no means sparing in expense when repairing or rebuilding their houses and within the past few years new parsonages had appeared at Timsbury, Dunkerton, Radstock, Writhlington and Midsomer Norton. The process gathered momentum in the succeeding years and bankrupted some incumbents whose ideas were bigger than their pockets, in the process. Four years after Skinner had watched the building of the parsonage at Priston, the perpetual curate of Forest Hill, a little village to the east of Oxford, began to build a house for the benefice which he described as 'one of the most convenient and complete places of residence in the Diocese' when it was finished in 1830. Unfortunately, however, it had run the incumbent into debt and in 1834 one of his creditors, who was in fact his own lawyer, put him into prison for eight months for owing under ten pounds. Upon his release he struggled on but, not being able to shake off the millstone of his financial obligations from round his neck, was back again in prison in 1843 in the gaol at Oxford Castle. Four years later he was deprived of his living by the energetic Wilberforce, Bishop of Oxford, and though he protested at his deprivation and sought other livings, both his protests and his pleadings fell on deaf ears. He died eventually in 1853 in the debtors' gaol to which the building of the parsonage at Forest Hill had brought him.[4] Some two dozen miles from Forest Hill, on the other side of Oxford, the rector of Great Rollright pulled down his old rectory in 1849 and began to build a new one, appearing from time to time with the demand, 'Give me air—give me space! Enlarge it here! Enlarge it there!' becoming so financially embarrassed as a result that he could not leave the house except to take services on Sunday and then only by way of the kitchen garden. In church one Sunday morning in 1851 having announced his text, 'Forgive us our debts as we forgive our debtors', he disappeared into the vestry and was seen no more.[5]

Most of the clergy, however, counted the cost more carefully before building great houses or living in them and so avoided bankruptcy, though they might find the grandeur expensive to maintain. Pluckley Rectory in Kent was a mansion belonging to a wealthy living, but when Ashton Oxenden was appointed rector in 1848, from whence he moved twenty-one years later on becoming Bishop of Montreal, he found that its upkeep, together with a kitchen garden of nearly an acre surrounded by a wall, had nearly emptied the pocket of his predecessor. It is not surprising that he maintained in a book of advice to the clergy that some parsonages had become too large and too luxurious, aping the hall and the squire. R. W. Evans, who had written a similar book in

1842 while vicar of Tarvin in Cheshire, moving from there to Heversham where he built a new vicarage for the view and where he was also for a few years Archdeacon of Westmorland, said the same. Others, if they did not object to the size of the new houses, took exception to their situation, finding that they were frequently too far from the church. J. J. Blunt, who had been Lady Margaret Professor of Divinity at Cambridge, remarked, 'I cannot omit observing, that we most certainly should not have had so many modern parsonages erected at most unseemly distances from the churches, for the sake of the view, or the like, as we now have—(to the great hindrance of religion)—had more frequent Services within the Church walls been customary, and tied the clergyman down to the scene of his work.'[6] The bishops, who might have suggested a limitation on the size of vicarages and rectories and have had some say in their situation, were hardly in a position to do so since they lived in palaces and castles sometimes set in deep countryside. The Bishop of Worcester gave the old episcopal palace in Worcester to the Dean, spent seven thousand pounds on Hartlebury Castle in 1846 and enjoyed living there though it was far from Worcester and the centre of his diocese. Bishops could hardly complain, then, if incumbents saw themselves as an ecclesiastical version of the landed gentry and, so long as they built within their parish, lived where they liked.

Not all the beneficed clergy lived in mansions, many of them being content, if not with a Diogenes tub, at least with a house of more modest dimensions. Patrick Brontë and his remarkable family occupied the parsonage at Haworth and considered it adequate though it was not large and had been built in 1740. Mrs. Gaskell described it in her life of Charlotte Brontë;

The Parsonage stands at right angles to the road, facing down upon the church; so that, in fact, parsonage, church and belfried school-house, form three sides of an irregular oblong, of which the fourth is open to the fields and moors that lie beyond. The area of this oblong is filled up by a crowded churchyard, and a small garden or court in front of the clergyman's house. As the entrance to this from the road is at the side, the path goes round the corner into the little plot of ground. Underneath the windows is a narrow flower-border, carefully tended in days of yore, although only the most hardy plants could be made to grow there. Within the stone wall, which keeps out the surrounding churchyard, are bushes of elder and lilac; the rest of the ground is occupied by a square grass plot and a gravel walk. The house is of grey stone, two stories high, heavily roofed with flags, in order to resist the winds that might strip off a lighter covering. It appears to have been built about a hundred years ago, and to consist of four rooms on each storey; the two windows on the right (as the visitor stands, with his back to the church, ready to enter in at the front door) belonging to Mr. Brontë's study, the two on the left to the family sitting-room. Everything about the place tells of the most dainty order, the most exquisite cleanliness. The door-steps are spotless; the small old-fashioned window-panes glitter like looking-glass. Inside and outside of that house cleanliness goes up into its essence, purity.[7]

The house was austere, with sanded floors, sparse furnishing and, in the earlier years of the Brontë occupation, no wallpaper. Miss Branwell, the aunt, went about the house in pattens, for fear of catching cold, clicking up and down the uncarpeted stone stairs, while two servants only, Tabby and Martha, looked after the family's needs. Dinner, which was at two, was often taken in the kitchen with Tabby, for Mr. Brontë, having trouble with his digestion, preferred to eat alone: the Brontë daughters debated their works in the dining-room. The proximity of the churchyard, jammed with rain-blackened tombstones, made the parsonage unhealthy and the water suspect, but though Mr. Brontë made forcible representations to the Board of Health, which recommended that future interments be forbidden, a new graveyard opened on the hillside, and a water supply made available to each house, nothing was done because the ratepayers scotched the scheme. The nearness of large numbers of the dead to the living affected parsonages elsewhere that had been built near the churchyard wall. The old rectory at St. Mary's, Newington, London, was roomy and half-ruined in 1869 when a future Archbishop of York, W. D. Maclagan, was appointed to the living and found that the water from the rectory's wells was clear, sparkling and poisonous, tainted by churchyard drainage.

Another unhealthy rectory was Kingsley's at Eversley, which had been built on low ground, with the churchyard six feet above the living-rooms, and liable to flooding. Kingsley enjoyed keeping the floods at bay, working once till one in the morning by candlelight, breaking holes in the wall with a pickaxe to prevent all being washed away, calling it 'fun'; but it necessitated expensive measures, first the filling in of the ponds and then new drainage, for which Kingsley asked help from the patron but received none. The rectory was a rambling seventeenth-century house, with parts dating from the fifteenth century, with many steps up and down and odd corners and cupboards. The study had a vast fireplace which contained footholds for the chimney-sweeps and Mary Kingsley remembered its 'lattice window (in later years altered to a bay), its great heavy door, studded with large projecting nails, opening upon the garden; its brick floor covered with matting; its shelves of heavy old folios, with a fishing-rod, or landing-net, or insect net leaning against them; on the table, books, writing materials, sermons, manuscripts, proofs, letters, reels, feathers, fishing-flies, clay pipes, tobacco'.[8] There was a suggestion at Eversley that a new rectory might be built but there were difficulties with the patron and the Kingsleys stayed on there, moving out sometimes for the winter when the dampness became insupportable, for many of these old houses were low-lying and inconvenient. The vicarage at Kenwyn-cum-Kea, about a mile from Truro, was a large, stone-built house but, as Cornishmen said, built 'agin the country', with ground rising directly at the back of it so that the study was dangerously damp; though the health of one of its incumbents was not impaired, however, for E. H. Browne, who had long legs and a poor circulation, held the living seven years and went on to be bishop, first of Ely, then of Winchester, before dying at the age of eighty.

A parson, therefore, finding himself with a rambling rectory full of mildew or a vicarage that vexed his wife, might gain the assent of his patron to pull it down and build anew according to his taste. If such a man were only in his twenties when appointed to his living, and many were, he could look forward to thirty, forty or even fifty years within the parish, as many did, making it worthwhile to build afresh. A rector was appointed to Berwick in Sussex in 1846, who rebuilt the rectory, being his own architect. When he died sixty years later he was still the rector so had had good use of the house. His parish witnessed only one institution to the living in the nineteenth century for his predecessor had been appointed in 1797 and had held it forty-nine years. To these new houses replacing older ones must be added others, built either in new parishes or districts, or in parishes that had had no parsonage before, making a considerable number. Such vicarages and rectories were substantial, commodious, but not necessarily over-large. The Ecclesiastical Commissioners made rules that a house likely to qualify for one of their grants should have, if possible, two sitting-rooms, a study, kitchen and scullery, all about sixteen feet by fourteen feet, though study and scullery could be a little less; together with a minimum of five bedrooms and a pantry or china closet, larder, W.C., linen closet, wine and beer cellar (did the temperance movement know?) dustbins and coalhouse. At first the Commissioners employed their own architect, William Railton, who designed Nelson's Column in Trafalgar Square, London, and he produced a series of uninteresting parsonages in the Elizabethan or Italian style, but usually the Italian, for it was found to be the cheaper. The work was found to be too much for one man in the 1840s so the Commissioners let local architects into the field and in consequence a wider variety of design appeared, with the Gothic revival making its influence felt.

In the eighteenth century Horace Walpole had put into the Holbein Chamber at Strawberry Hill a chimney-piece copied chiefly from Archbishop Warham's tomb in Canterbury Cathedral and a ceiling 'coved and fretted in quatrefoil compartments, with roses at the intersection, all in papier-mâché'. The first murmurs of the Gothic revival, then, were romantic, rococo and a little flimsy, for it was not in origin a religious movement at all; and even when churches came to be erected in considerable numbers in the Gothic style early in the nineteenth century, with grants made by Parliament, the decision to use Gothic was one of taste rather than economics or religion, for the cost of classical and Gothic churches was about the same and both styles were recognised as suitable for churches. The Oxford Movement, however, took the Gothic revival under its wing and so effectively baptised it that the Victorians came to feel that Gothic was the only true style of Christian architecture. Churches must be built in the idiom of the Middle Ages and, if churches should be built so, then why not parsonages, too? They might not contain fireplaces copied from tombs or papier-mâché ceiling, for these were frivolous conceits; but they should have that about them which proclaimed their ecclesiastical purpose so that the passer-by would see both the house in which the vicar lived and the church in which he led the worship and know by their common style that they belonged together.

There had been back in the eighteenth century parsonages that had borrowed the idiom of Strawberry Hill, like the rectory of Charlton Mackrell in Somerset, built about 1792, which had a Gothic porch and, inside, a Gothic screen between the hall and staircase. In 1837 Hawker at Morwenstow built himself a vicarage adapted from a plan for 'a Clergyman's house on a moderate scale' in which 'frugality may be exercised without the appearance of poverty' according to the book of *Designs for Parsonage Houses* by T. F. Hunt, from which the plan came; and to the new building he added chimneys in the shape of the towers of churches with which he had been associated and made the kitchen chimney like his mother's tomb. In the 1840s, however, this light-hearted treatment of Gothic detail began to be frowned upon and the *Ecclesiologist*, which was the periodical that contended that all things Christian should be Gothic and spread the message that parsonages should partake of the stable and permanent character of the Church itself, judging them accordingly in its pages. Vicarages and rectories began to appear, therefore, with porches that were church porches, chimney-stacks like buttresses running up outside walls, roofs steep and slated, staircases in turrets rising into spirelets, and windows that were arched or, perhaps, boasted trefoil heads of brown sand-stone as at St. John's Vicarage at Middlesborough, built about 1865. If Butterfield designed such a house, then, like his churches, polychromatic bricks arranged in zigzags, bands and lozenges, formed intriguing designs across its façade. These houses of the Gothic revival were neither graceful nor elegant; rather, they were unsymmetrical, sombre and sub-stantial, suiting the life-style that the clergy who lived in them were encouraged to adopt, for the clergy were exhorted to cultivate a gravity of manner which it was thought fitted their calling. Oxenden maintained like many others that the every-day life of the minister should be solemn and gave a warning that in society especially this needed to be borne in mind.

But no movement lasts for ever. Towards the end of the nineteenth century, then, the Gothic revival lost its momen-tum and parsonages began to appear that had been influenced by Philip Webb's Red House at Bexley Heath and others like it. Domestic, unassuming, tile-hung, rough cast houses were built, inspired by cottages and farmhouses that were con-venient to live in and without pretension, like the Cotswold-style vicarage at All Saints, Westbrook, Margate, in brick and Kentish rag with windows closely set, in the 1890s. No longer was Gothic supreme: neo-Queen Anne, mock Tudor, any style was possible at the turn of the century for the clergyman who needed a new house for his benefice and he could choose according to his fancy.

The Reformation had opened the floodgates of matrimony to the clergy of the Anglican church so that the majority of parsonages came to be occupied by the incumbent with his wife and children. These were family houses in which the wives of the clergy exercised much influence, and even a bachelor vicar might well have a sister or a niece to keep house for him. But the Victorian Church saw the arrival of celibate anglo-catholic clergy who, if they were incumbents, might occupy a parsonage that was more the headquarters of the parish and the nerve centre of its activities than a house for living in. Father Dolling, a remarkable Irishman with weak eyes, accepted the charge of the Winchester College Mission at St. Agatha's, Landport, and for ten years exercised a memorable ministry in the slums of Portsmouth. His first parsonage there was joined to a gymnasium, which could be reached without going into the street and in which a number of cubicles were constructed for sailors on leave who, when they quarrelled at night, could be quelled by Dolling's speedy arrival. The gymnasium itself had once been a Baptist chapel and beneath its floor rested the remains of two of its ministers, which were not exhumed when the chapel closed, so that dancing and athletics were carried on over their bones. Outside there was a large slaughter-yard, which sent out a strong smell and attracted the bluebottles.[9] Not so dramatically as this, Richard Jefferies painted a picture of the hard-working vicar of a country town oblivious to his own comfort and surely unmarried, for in the study 'the furniture, of oak, is plain and spare to the verge of a gaunt severity, and there is not one single picture-frame on the wide expanse of wall. On the table are a few books and some letters, with foreign postmarks, and addressed in the crabbed handwriting of continental scholars. Over the table a brazen lamp hangs suspended by a slender chain. In a corner are some fragments of stone mouldings and wood carvings like the panel of an ancient pew. There are no shelves and no bookcase.'[10] Contrast this with the parish of St. Jude's, Whitechapel, London, where the vicarage was small, dark and inconvenient yet had drawing-room curtains of primrose silk against walls the colour of opals, wallpapers by William Morris and pheasant sometimes to eat in the dining-room, for at St. Jude's there was a redoubtable vicar's wife in the person of Henrietta Barnett.

Some celibate clergy turned their parsonages into clergy

houses and gathered their curates within their walls to live a communal life of considerable austerity. At St. Alban's, Holborn, reporters observed that the curates practised celibacy in the open street—the phrase was used elsewhere—for they, like their vicars, were single and anglo-catholic. The meals at St. Alban's clergy house consisted chiefly of very large pieces of beef cooked at long intervals, producing much cold meat which, with potatoes, bread and cheese, constituted the bulk of the fare. Raisins appeared on festivals. Father Mackonochie, the vicar, would rush in when his curates were nearly finishing their meal, bolt his food in three minutes and then rush off for another engagement while a cat called Blobbs might perch on the shoulder of Father Stanton, the famous curate, during dinner. Not all clergy houses were to be found in anglo-catholic parishes, however, for the one at Portsea served a parish where ceremonial was minimal in the days of Edgar Jacob, who was responsible for establishing a staff of ten curates and taking them to live with him at the vicarage. There, on a Sunday evening, at supper, black coats were exchanged for college blazers, bread was hurled across the table and the vicar occasionally found himself under it. When Cosmo Gordon Lang succeeded Jacob as vicar in 1895 the high spirits on Sunday evenings vanished and a more disciplined way of life established. Cod on Fridays and plenty of cold mutton provided a monotonous menu. The vicarage contained no bathroom and everyone had a cold tub in the morning in his own room. The curates respected Lang, called him 'sir', and when they wanted to see him made an appointment as though they were parishioners.

Such intensive use of a vicarage was rare and only to be found in a few town parishes. More common was the parish that did not have a vicarage at all, for in spite of all endeavours a number of livings remained without a parsonage, leaving their incumbents to fend for themselves. The visitation returns of the diocese of York in 1865 showed not only that the vicar of Adlingfleet was perpetually enjoying the waters of Bath, that the rector of Londesborough was the Earl of Carlisle who had put a curate in sole charge of his parish since 1840, and that the rector of Rawmarsh lived in Florence; but that of the five hundred and seventy-seven distinct benefices in the diocese, one hundred and seventy remained without parsonages, so that the clergy appointed to these one hundred and seventy livings must find their own house to live in, and this might not be easy as the case of Ketteringham in Norfolk shows. In 1835 William Wayte Andrew was presented to the benefice of Ketteringham, worth less than two hundred pounds a year, and found himself in a small parish of two hundred people or so, with a manor house, twenty-eight cottages, but no parsonage for the incumbent. At first he rented a house a mile from Ketteringham church, holding it on a short lease, but when the house was sold to Sir John Boileau, who had also bought the Hall at Ketteringham, Andrew had to move out, Boileau having promised it to another. But where to go? As the vicar surveyed the possibilities within three miles of Ketteringham church, which was the limit that the bishop permitted for his residence, he could see nothing that was suitable. Borrowing a wheel with which to measure the distance, he walked to a house at Wreningham, ejaculating as he walked, 'Lord, hinder me if not for Thy glory' and found it further than the three miles he was allowed. In July 1841, the bishop withdrew the stipulation on the distance from the church, announcing that he was prepared to license the nearest house available, which opened the wider possibility that Andrew might live in Wymondham three and a half miles away, or perhaps in Norwich if nothing else suitable and nearer could be found. At this moment a house at Hethersett came on the market at a price of four thousand pounds, a small house not in the parish of Ketteringham and yet conveniently close to it and its church. Andrew was not short of money and could well afford the sum asked; but he thought the price too high and his religious principles prevented him from extravagance. In August the house was auctioned at Norwich and Andrew bid three thousand five hundred and twenty-five pounds only to be told that the reserve price was four thousand pounds and that it was accordingly withdrawn. Two days later the auctioneer came to him and offered him the house for three thousand seven hundred pounds. He refused to go beyond three thousand six hundred pounds but this was in the end accepted and Andrew and his wife went to live at Wood Hall, Hethersett, which was their home for more than forty years. When he resigned the living in 1887 there was still no parsonage at Ketteringham.[11]

Another vicar who did not live in a vicarage was visited by Francis Kilvert in 1872, while he was curate at Clyro in Radnorshire. He found the vicar living in a little grey hut built of rough dry stone without mortar in a green sunny little cwm and when he entered found;

> there was a wild confusion of litter and rubbish almost choking and filling up all available space. The floor had once been of stone but was covered thick and deep with an accumulation of the dirt and peat dust of years. The furniture consisted of two wooden saddle-seated chairs polished smooth by the friction of continual sessions, and one of them without a back. A four-legged dressing table littered with broken bread and meat, crumbs, dirty knives and forks, glasses, plates, cups and saucers in squalid hugger-mugger confusion. No table cloth. No grate. The hearth foul with cold peat ashes, broken bricks and dust, under the great wide open chimney through which stole down a faint ghastly sickly light. In heaps and piles upon the floor were old books, large Bibles, commentaries, old-fashioned religious disputations, C. M. S. Reports and odd books of all sorts, Luther on the Galatians, etc. The floor was further encumbered with beams and logs of wood, flour pans covered over, and old chests. All the other articles of food were hung up on pot hooks some from the ceiling, some in the chimney out of the way of the rats. The squalor, the dirt, the dust, the foulness and wretchedness of the place were indescribable, almost inconceivable. And in this cabin thus lives the Solitary of Lanbedr, the Revd. John Price, Master of Arts of Cambridge University and Vicar of Llanbedr Painscastle.[12]

Yet he did duty in his church and kindly and assiduously visited the sick so that one of his parishioners at least died very
happy.

The hut clearly had no servants but this was an extreme
case of a vicar withdrawn from the world who lived alone.
Most incumbents had servants, some many of them. At Old
Alresford Francis North, Earl of Guilford, son of Bishop
Brownlow North who occupied the See of Winchester from
1781 to 1820, was the rector; and at Old Alresford Place he,
the Countess and five children lived with seventeen servants,
according to a census of 1845. In the days of George Sumner,
appointed his successor in 1851 to this wealthy living, it took
one servant all the morning to trim and to refill the forty oil
lamps that were needed in the house, while George Sumner's
wife, Mary, founder of the Mothers' Union, is reputed never
to have put on her own stockings in her life. Little wonder,
then, that in 1851 domestic servants were one of the two
largest groups of the population, for no gentleman's house
was complete without a cook, a housemaid and a gardener. So
we must picture parsonages inhabited by incumbents and
their families, together with some servants who slept in the
attics and lived in the kitchen if there was not a servants' hall.
In the parsonage the servants could act sometimes as inter-
mediaries between their clerical master and the poor and
needy of the parish, for, given the social stratification of society in the nineteenth century, there was a great gulf fixed
between a vicar and the poorest of his parishioners. The poor
would not think of going to the front door of the vicarage but
they were prepared to go round to the back and there they
would put their needs to cook or housemaid who might advise
them and, if need be, go and tell the master of the problem
that the caller brought. On a May day in 1871 Francis Kilvert
called on the vicar of Glascwm, knocked on the front door
and waited for some time before anyone came. It appeared
that the girl was quite a new servant and did not know where
the front door was, village visitors always going round the
back, and so, hearing a knock, she had gone to the back door
and found no one. The vicar enlightened her.

Servants brought comfortable living to those who employed them, but they could be a cause of anxiety, too, to their employers, especially if the females among them were discovered to be with child, for this was more unfortunate in a parsonage, where moral standards were presumed to be high, than in other gentlemen's houses. In 1859 an unmarried servant at the rectory of Poughill, near Bude in Cornwall, gave birth to a child whom she murdered. The police were called, the servant taken into custody, and an inquest followed, at which she was convicted and imprisoned. The rector seemed less concerned with the sin of the servant than with his own inconvenience, but it was an unfortunate incident.

Servants, however, seemed indispensable to the average nineteenth-century incumbent who, if he were well-to-do, lived comfortably enough, benefiting also from the household improvements that were being made everywhere at that time. Water-closets made their appearance. Benjamin Newton returned to his rectory at Wath near Ripon in 1816 to inspect one that had been built in his absence, but this and others like it would have been insanitary affairs, for the flush toilet as we know it dates from about 1889. The vicarage of St. Mary's, Newbury in 1855 had a W.C. on each floor, with cisterns, two sinks and a tap for housemaids, while the plans for the house at St. Mary Abbots, Kensington (1876) had a bathroom upstairs, and in it a grate and back boiler to heat the water on the spot. Before that, however, Charles Kingsley had installed central heating at Eversley, urged on by Fanny, his extravagant wife. In 1865 Charles wrote to her in Bournemouth from the rectory, wondering what to do with his fourth child, Grenville, who had been sent home because the sun on the beach was too much for him, and suggesting that he go to his grandmother's cottage.

I wish you would send Grenville to the cottage on Saturday. All the back of the house is open. He will surely catch a cold as can be. Moreover it would be physically so dreadfully dangerous. No floors, open rafters, no stairs, open pits everywhere and bricks and wood continually dropping.

And if he was kept away from the work it would be a per-petual irritation to him. We have settled all the pipes. We are going to take them into the W.C. and warm it thoroughly. I believe more colds and sciatica are caught there than anywhere. I know how a cold W.C. affects me.[13]

Warmth and light were being more appreciated. Hawker at Morwenstow was delighted at the radiance of his first oil lamp in 1858, but as late as 1910 Bishop King of Lincoln sent a message from his death-bed to a young architect that he should build houses with sunny rooms for the clergy.

Parsonages naturally enough reflected the interests and idiosyncrasies of their occupants. Fox-hunting parsons hung on their walls relics of the chase; learned parsons had books in their studies and elsewhere in the house; gardening parsons had splendid lawns and flower-beds. Fox-hunting parsons were numerous in the early nineteenth century, when it was estimated that twenty clergy in the diocese of Exeter kept packs of hounds, including in that number John Froude of Knowstone. Bishop Phillpotts summoned him to Exeter, but since he refused to go the bishop visited him one winter's morning to find him sitting wrapped up over the fire. The vicar ordered brandy and water hot and strong for his Lord-ship but the bishop declined it and tried to explain the pur-pose of his visit, at which Froude cut him short, saying, 'It's my only doctor, my lord, is a drop of brandy; and if I had but taken it when I got my chill, I shouldn't now be as I be, deaf as a haddock, and nursing this fire like an old woman.' The story, perhaps, has been improved in the telling, but the bishop's diary does record under the date July 19th, 1831, what was presumably another visit, 'went to Knowstone. Mr. Froude ill in bed. The church good; house fair; in dining-room six foxes' brushes, two of them bell-pulls with a fox engraved, and Tally-ho! upon them.'[14]

Scholarly clergymen had their books and might display their learning more prominently, as Christopher Wordsworth did at Stanford-in-the-Vale-cum-Goosey, near the Vale of the White Horse. There he greatly enlarged the vicarage after undertaking the charge of the parish in 1850, and had written up numerous inscriptions in Latin, Greek and English, including among them, 'Whether ye eat or drink . . . do all to the glory of God' (in English) in the dining-room; 'Martha, Martha' (in Greek) over the store-room closet; and a quotation from the second of Paul's letters to the Corinthians (in Latin) over the dressing-room door, 'We do not wish to be unclothed but clothed upon'. Some clothes were presumably taken off at the vicarage of Wymeswold, near Loughborough, where Henry Alford spent two hours every evening educating his children. 'He was also particularly attentive to the development of their bodily powers: and a room was elaborately fitted up for the practice of gymnastics, in which he was frequently their teacher.'

There were many happy children in parsonages, but there were also unhappy ones as Samuel Butler's *The Way of All Flesh* testifies. Some clerical homes could be oppressive, for Victorian parents had high ideals and demanded much from their children. When Archbishop Benson was headmaster of Wellington College, near Wokingham, his children were in awe and fear of him, for he wanted his pupils to see in his own family models for them to follow. Mercifully Mrs. Benson was adored by all her children and the oppressiveness was tempered by the shrewd and capable mother with a delightful sense of humour. Baring-Gould's uncle, Alexander, was vicar of a newly erected church in Wolverhampton and very envangelical; Baring-Gould went to spend a fortnight with him in 1853. One rainy day he and his sister romped round the dining-room table and in the evening at family prayers they were prayed for before the servants that they might be freed from the spirit of levity. Coming away from the house they sang in the cab on the way to the station and the cabman said 'not surprised to hear you singing, sir, coming away from that idiot asylum. A few weeks ago I took away two young ladies, Misses Ireland, and they frolicked like wild cats, and broke one of the panes of glass in my cab window.'

The outside walls of the parsonage might be clothed with ivy, much beloved of the Victorians, who encouraged it to grow up and over the walls of churches also, in spite of the damage it might inflict upon the fabric of the building against which it climbed. An American visitor asked Keble at Hursley for a piece of the ivy overhanging the vicarage porch and Keble, amused and a little mystified, reached up and cut him a long spray. 'You may laugh,' said the American, 'but there are people at home in the States who would give me large sums of money for every leaf.' Gardens, with the help of cheap labour, were well kept; a neat, close-cut lawn running up to the churchyard wall with well-trimmed flower-beds, a terrace perhaps, a shrubbery, a paddock and a fruit and vege-table garden together with a conservatory or greenhouse, graced the surroundings of many country parsonages, though in towns the amount of land available was usually con-siderably less and some houses gave straight on to the street. In the country it was possible to specialise in some branch of horticulture, which many incumbents did. The vicar appointed to the parish of Honingham, near Norwich, in 1882 was much given to the growing of orchids, it was noted, though his predecessor in the living had been addicted to the rearing of poultry. At Whittington, seventeen miles north of Shrewsbury, Walsham How cultivated a variety of ferns in the rocky banks of a small stream in the rectory garden; at Shir-ley, near Croydon, a vicar raised the Shirley poppy in a garden inspired by the landscapes of Capability Brown; and at the rectory of Wilton, Salisbury, Canon Olivier, rector from 1867 to 1912, picked two hundred or more roses on a summer's morning, the loveliest of which he displayed in individual vases in green wood showcases in the large, cool hall. The lawns were used for archery, tennis and croquet and for bazaars. In 1870 the vicarage garden at Hardwick in Herefordshire was the scene of a bazaar for Home Missions, where a band banged and blasted away and people ran in all directions with large pictures, bags, rugs, cushions, smoking caps and other articles, asking everyone they met to join in raffling for them. At five o'clock there was universal tea in a tent with long tables and forms, but no teaspoons so that Kil-vert had to stir his tea and cut his bread and butter with his newly acquired paper-knife. Half-an-hour later the Bishop of Hereford began to speak, spoke for an hour, disclosed that he was no orator and had to be reminded that he would miss the last train home if he did not stop.[15] A more sinister event was the murder of the rector of Frimley in his rectory garden during the unrest in the countryside in the autumn of 1850.

The number of animals, welcome and unwelcome, that inhabited parsonages was considerable. The clergy house at St. Alban's, Holborn, had a cat; Hawker at Morwenstow was reputed to have had nine or ten of them, who followed him to church and careered round the chancel during the service. Dogs were common and could be fierce. Emily Brontë had a fierce dog, Keeper, and there was another dog, Flossy, at the parsonage. More unusual was the white owl that lived in the parsonage at Southrop, which Keble occupied before moving to Hursley, for the owl had a favourite perch on the top of the kitchen dresser were he slept all day, snoring loudly to the alarm of the housekeeper. Hawker had at one time a couple of deer, for a visiting clergyman of evangelical principles was pinned to the ground by the antlers of one of them and had to be rescued by him. And then there were the rats, which plagued many vicarages and rectories, such as the rectory at Camerton where the rector struck at the wainscoting of his bedroom with the poker, but frightened them not at all for, returning to the charge, they seemed as though they would eat through the wood. At the rectory at Langley Burrell, making a horrible noise at night, they seemed sometimes to be pulling down the walls and sometimes to be playing bowls and skittles. At Whittington Rectory in the 1840s a fox, very odorous, had been chained to a kennel near the front door and was shut up whenever the hounds met in the neighbourhood.

The timetable of a parsonage as far as meals were concerned followed the pattern that was observed in the houses of the gentry. In the days of Jane Austen breakfast was at ten, in consequence of which many activities took place before that meal. Sometime in the middle of the day there was a luncheon of a fair size, but taken informally and not usually in the dining-room, at which cold meat frequently made an appearance; at Mansfield parsonage 'the sandwich tray and Dr. Grant doing the honours of it' were in the same room as Mrs. Grant and her tambour frame and Mary and her harp and her admirer. Dinner, the big gastronomic occasion of the day, came in the late afternoon and varied with the fashion of the diners. At the parsonage at Mansfield it was at four thirty, but people of great sophistication dined later, at five or six o'clock, or even at six thirty. After dinner the ladies retired to the drawing-room and drank coffee before the gentlemen joined them and then, after a considerable interval, came tea. If supper was served, and often it was not, it would be a light meal taken like lunch, upon a tray, though the old-fashioned liked to have the cloth laid since that had been the fashion in the eighteenth century.

By Victorian times breakfast at parsonages had become earlier, for at Morwenstow, Eversley and Old Alresford breakfast was at eight. The dinner hour varied as it had varied twenty years before; at Morwenstow it was at one o'clock, at Eversley Kingsley suggested that it should be at five, while Hook at Leeds dined at three, as did the Sumner family at Old Alresford. The energetic clergyman did not start his day with breakfast at eight, however, for he had been up long before. Kingsley thought it right to rise at six and to have family prayers at seven thirty before breakfast, while W. F. Hook in his younger days would rise at four, though he told a young clergyman that he might not find this suited him. H. P. Liddon thought that the latest hour for rising should be six in the summer and seven in the winter and that the clergyman on getting out of bed should immediately thank God for his preservation, remembering that on an average twelve thousand souls would have that very night passed to their account. While dressing he should recite Psalm 51, the *Te Deum* or some other Christian hymn and then spend half-an-hour in meditation.[16] Between breakfast and dinner the incumbents went about their parish duties, visiting their parishioners, teaching in their schools, taking services in their churches, reading, writing and relaxing. At Morwenstow, breakfast was followed by morning prayer and visiting, and after their early dinner Hawker read to Mrs. Hawker while she sewed or knitted. At four he went to church for evening service and at five there was tea. In that remote part of Cornwall the letters and newspapers did not arrive till then and the evening was spent with them until bed at about eleven o'clock. In the country, evenings were usually spent at home, since moving about was difficult in the dark, and Kingsley romantically pictured these times at his rectory with Fanny when, after dinner, 'we will . . . draw and feed our intellect and fancy all evening with your head on my bosom and our lips meeting every now and again to tell each other something that is too deep for words. Then family prayers and bed at eleven.'

It must not be assumed that the clergy were always in their parishes, even if John Keble thought that the trivial round and common task were all that men required, giving room for self-denial and providing a road to bring them nearer to God. There were parsonages, certainly, where the daily routine went on more or less unchanged year after year, since some incumbents rarely left their parishes. Bartholomew Edwards, rector of Ashill in Norfolk, had been a great horseman and rider to hounds but came to feel that hunting was unfitting for a clergyman and gave it up. He was absent from his parish church on three Sundays only in the thirty years before 1889, when he died within nine days of his hundredth birthday. Others, however, were away frequently from their parishes, sometimes for months at a time, either because of their other duties and interests, or because of their ill-health or the ill-health of their wives or children, or because they were indolent; an absence made possible by those helots of the Victorian Church, the assistant curates, who were readily obtainable and would be engaged at a reasonable price to take parochial duty. B. J. Armstrong, devoted vicar of East Dereham, was accustomed to take two or three weeks holiday in May or June and a month or more around August. Longer periods of absence were necessary for incumbents who were residentiary canons, for this entailed them in being away from their parishes three months in the year while they did their turn of duty in their cathedrals; and even longer absences were required by the few who combined an incumbency with a professorship, as Kingsley did for a time. While William Lake was at Huntspill his name was suggested in 1860 for the Chichele Professorship of Modern History at Oxford, but he declined it since he thought it undesirable to be away eight months in the year from his fair-sized parish, leaving a curate in charge. As it was, he reckoned that his duties as preacher at the Chapel Royal, Whitehall, his eduational work and his other commitments kept him away from Huntspill five months out of twelve. Nor did parishioners like their vicar to be frequently absent, as one of E. H. Browne's curates at Heavitree, Devon, noted: 'he is to return tomorrow, in time for a parish dinner at the Horse and Groom. No very pleasant form of martyrdom for any vicar, but for him especially unpleasant, as he hates public speaking, and as the captious part of the parish are angry at his being so much away from the church.'[17]

Parishioners were coming to expect higher standards from their clergy, but sometimes they had to tolerate their lengthy absences, especially during the winter months when they would set off for the south coast resorts or go abroad. Oxenden found the wear and tear of the work at Pluckley, with its population of eight hundred, so overwhelming that in the autumn of 1863 he went with his sister for a few months stay in Torquay, putting the parish into the hands of a curate; and when he returned to England from being Bishop of Montreal he found the winter so damp and trying that he left the parish of St. Stephen's, Canterbury, and resided for six months in Biarritz. Knowing that he would have to do the same the following year, he then resigned the living. Many incumbents went abroad and wrote voluminous accounts of their European travels, reporting with mixed fascination and horror on the practices that they observed in the catholic churches of the Continent. In 1866 Brooke Lambert became vicar of St. Mark's, Whitechapel, where he had been curate. It was a difficult parish of eleven thousand in which he had to face an epidemic of cholera that involved the burying of forty-four corpses in one day. As a result, broken in health, he resigned the living four years later and went abroad with the vicar of St. Philip's, Stepney, who was also sick, and there met the vicar of Rainhill, Lancashire, who was also convalescing.

There were other incumbents who, though resident in their parishes, were virtually useless because they were mad or senile. Mark James Pattison, father of Mark Pattison, was rector of Hauxwell in Yorkshire for forty years from 1825 to 1865. Partially insane, he spent two years and more in a mental home in York in the 1830s. His favourite reading was *Debrett* and his favourite occupation the tormenting of his wife and twelve children, refusing to speak to his daughters for weeks on end and sulking in the bookroom at the bottom of the stairs. He neglected his parish but used the pulpit to denounce the family. When the Bill to enable the clergy to resign their livings was being considered in 1870, Bishop Wilberforce sent a draft to Lord Westbury who observed that the draft's reference to diseases of the mind presented a difficulty since there was no such thing and that he had not met a clergyman with a mind, except Bishop Wilberforce.

But, in the end, the mad, the senile, the good and the bad incumbent moved or died and the parsonage was vacated for another. The incoming incumbent demanded that his predecessor or his predecessor's estate should meet the cost of repairs to the house and other benefice buildings, which led not infrequently to disputes as to what should be done. Judgment in the case of Wise *v.* Metcalfe in 1829 reaffirmed earlier precedents and laid down that an incumbent must repair, restore and rebuild his parsonage and its outbuildings, but that he need not do this until it became necessary and that he had no obligation to make improvements or to decorate interiors. In 1862 the new rector of Bulwick in Nothamptonshire took over a rectory that had a well, but was without a drain or a pump for drawing water, the previous incumbent having fetched his water in a water cart from a brook. The surveyors agreed on the sum of one hundred and thirty pounds for the dilapidations but it was estimated that to put the house in good order would cost seven hundred pounds and there were the farm buildings, the glebe, and the chancel of the church to maintain. The new rector reckoned that he must pay one hundred pounds a year interest on the money that he had to borrow and to lay down three years' income for the work. The Ecclesiastical Dilapidations Act of 1871 provided for a compulsory survey of all benefice buildings at each vacancy of a living, to be administered by Queen Anne's Bounty; and this gave an impartial and standardised survey throughout the country, taking some of the heat out of the disputes between incumbents arriving and departing. It was not till 1923 that vicars and rectors had to make an annual payment to the Bounty to cover the cost of the repairs, which were to be undertaken every five years as a result of a quinquennial inspection.

NOTES

1 Hesketh Pearson, *The Smith of Smiths*, pp. 145, 271.
2 Alice Fairfax-Lucy, *Charlecote and the Lucys*, pp. 251, 310–15.
3 Alan Savidge, *The Parsonage in England*, pp. 119–20.
4 V. H. H. Green, *Oxford Common Room*, pp. 27–9.
5 Diana McClatchey, *Oxfordshire Clergy, 1777–1869*, pp. 26–7.
6 J. J. Blunt, *The Parish Priest*, p. 311.
7 Mrs. Gaskell, *Life of Charlotte Brontë*, pp. 3–4.
8 Mary Kingsley, *Charles Kingsley*, Vol. I, p. 302.
9 C. E. Osborne, *The Life of Father Dolling*, pp. 93–7.
10 Richard Jefferies, *Hodge and his Masters*, Vol. I, p. 162.
11 Owen Chadwick, *Victorian Miniature*, Ch. 3.
12 Francis Kilvert, *Diary*, July 3rd, 1872.
13 Susan Chitty, *The Beast and the Monk*, p. 256.
14 G. C. B. Davies, *Henry Phillpotts*, p. 152.
15 Francis Kilvert, *Diary*, August 29th, 1870.
16 H. P. Liddon, *Clerical Life and Work*, p. 42.
17 G. W. Kitchen, *Edward Harold Browne*, p. 236.

CHAPTER 4

The Church

AT EVERSLEY THE rectory looked out on to the red-brick tower
of the church, with four vanes atop, one of which permanently
disagreed with its neighbours—'a nonconformist from its
birth', said Kingsley. It seemed right that church and rectory
should go together, as they did in many places, for the incumbent's first duty was to his congregation that gathered Sunday
by Sunday in the church and came at other times for baptisms,
marriages and burials. Early in the nineteenth century such an
incumbent arriving for the first time in his living would have
found most probably a mediaeval church as the setting of
parochial worship, with a nave and chancel at least, with an
aisle or aisles probably, and boasting perhaps a chapel which
was the property of the squire and under which his forbears
were buried. The interior, however, would have presented an
aspect not at all mediaeval, for much had been done to dis-
guise the Gothic features of the building by inserting a flat
plaster ceiling beneath the pitched roof, glazing the windows
in the eighteenth-century manner and putting curtains to
them, adding a gallery or two and pews of Georgian wood-
work, and erecting a reading-desk and pulpit which rose high
into the air. In the nave this edifice of the 'three-decker pulpit', containing a seat for the parish clerk, a desk for the priest
from which the prayers were taken, and a pulpit at the highest
level, was clearly the focal point of the furnishing since the
pews faced it and it commanded as far as it was able, a view of

all parts of the building. In the chancel, forlorn, half-hidden and not frequently regarded, stood the Holy Table. The arrangement was a logical one, given the character of the services.

For the Sunday services were services of prayer and preaching and Bible readings as laid down in the *Book of Common Prayer*. On a Sunday morning the incumbent who 'did duty' went to his reading-desk, and the Clerk went to his; then they were off on a service that might last two hours, beginning with morning prayer, continuing with the litany and the first part of the communion service, and ending with the sermon. At Wath, near Ripon, the rector arrived in church on Sunday, October 25th, 1818, to find that the clerk had looked out the lessons and psalms for the service to be used in celebration of the King's accession, but he thought that considering the state of King George III, who was by now quite mad, these were best omitted; so they reverted to those that were set for the twenty-third Sunday after Trinity. In morning prayer this involved forty verses of Psalm 119, a short lesson from the book of the prophet Hosea and the substantial eleventh chapter, containing fifty-four verses, from the Gospel according to St. Luke, interspersed with confession, canticles, creed and collects. Then followed the litany and the ante-communion at which the congregation heard, in the epistle, how their bodies would one day be changed into bodies fashioned like the glorious body of their Saviour, and, in the gospel, the reply of their Lord when the Pharisees brought him a penny and asked if it were lawful to give tribute unto Caesar. After the Nicene Creed the rector ascended to the pulpit and addressed his people for half-an-hour or so, before dismissing them with his blessing. Probably there was no collection, though there had been one two months before when the rector had preached on the need of repairs to Chester Cathedral, had sent round the churchwardens before the blessing and so had collected the sum of thirty shillings by his eloquence. Metrical versions of the psalms, either that of Sternhold and Hopkins or that of Tate and Brady, would have been sung during the service, accompanied by a small church band and singers. The wor-

ship of the Church was not short, though it was shorter at
evening prayer, which was held in the afternoon, than in the
morning, and at evening prayer, in place of a sermon, there
might be the catechising of the children of the parish.

Long services in unheated churches had caused the laity to
seek protection from the cold as best they could by erecting
pews, as a parishioner at Haverstock in Essex did in 1616,
making a pew with a high wainscot or board in order 'to break
and keep off the wind that cometh out of the chancel'.[1] There
were the straight ones, with a seat along one side, and there
were the square ones, in which the occupants knelt on three
sides facing inwards, with the door on the fourth. The walls of
the pews were four or five feet high so that, when sitting, the
heads only of the occupants were visible over the top, yet they
could see the officiating minister who was high above them in
reading-desk or pulpit. The pews faced the pulpit and should
the pulpit be situated halfway down the nave then the pews
between it and the chancel looked towards it and not towards
the altar on which they turned their backs, with the result that
odd nooks and alleyways and crannies appeared all over a
church, though the apparently haphazard arrangement was a
practical one. This gave an element of mystery to the interior
which was full of surprises, especially to a child who could not
see over the side of a pew at all. Henry Phipps Denison
remembered being taken as a child to the church at Hobart,
Tasmania, where his father was the Governor. It was a mys-
terious place, for the pew the Governor and his family
occupied was reached from the vestry door without entering
the body of the church; and since it was a square pew, with a
curtain of eighteen inches round its top, the child, though he
had a good view of the pulpit and a more curtailed view of the
reading-desk, could not see the rest of the church and certainly not the altar, for when the clergyman went there his
voice appeared to come from a place that one had never seen
and could never see. When in 1855 his father moved to New
South Wales, the pews in the church there were not so high
and more was visible.[2] Vicars and rectors, however, could see
their congregations well from their commanding height and,

sometimes, as at Ravenstonedale, Westmorland, put their family on the top storey, just behind the pulpit, to keep an eye on things as well.

A long service considerably taxed the strength of the minister conducting it and it was not unknown for a rector, unable to stand because he had gout in his feet, to conduct the whole service on his knees.[3] But the service would have been longer, and the kneeling position impossible to maintain, if the communion itself had been frequently administered. However, it was not frequently administered in the early years of the nineteenth century, for the Church by and large took the direction of the Prayer Book that every parishioner should communicate at least three times in the year, of which Easter should be one, to mean that the administration of the sacrament was required only three or four times in the space of twelve months. The visitation returns of the diocese of Exeter in 1833 show that quarterly celebrations were customary in the country and monthly celebrations in the town; but as late as 1865 in the diocese of York almost half the parishes had less than twelve celebrations a year, and in the parish of Eastrington the vicar did not celebrate at Christmas or Michaelmas because the churchwardens had not provided wine. In the early years of the century, therefore, and for some time after that, altars were little used, and when they were and the sacrament was administered, difficulties arose because from many of the pews it was not possible to see the Holy Table. One practice that overcame the problem was the custom observed at the old parish church of Leeds where communicants went into the chancel for the communion itself, but the chancel at Leeds was eighty feet by sixty feet and could accommodate many people. Elsewhere the chancel was frequently too small for this practice to be followed and then the communicants had perforce to stay in their seats and come only to the altar at the administration of the sacrament, which meant that a priest at the altar, looking down the chancel and into the nave, had the eerie feeling that he and the parish clerk were alone in the church since all the other worshippers were invisible, hidden in their pews. The arrangement was not ideal but was tolerated on account of the infrequency of the service.

Altars, lying unused for long periods, suffered various indignities and acquired other functions than that for which they were designed. In 1861 B. J. Armstrong was disgusted to find at Swanton church a rat-trap on the altar, baited with a piece of bread, into which a sparrow had intruded his unfortunate neck, and he took the liberty of removing so painful an object. When J. C. Atkinson first visited the parish church of Danby-in-Cleveland, where he was to minister for forty years, he found 'the altar-table was not only rickety, and with one leg shorter than the other, and besides that, mean and worm-eaten, but it was covered with what it would have been a severe and sarcastic libel to call a piece of green baize; for it was in rags, and of any or almost any colour save the original green. And even that was not all! It was covered thickly over with stale crumbs. It seemed impossible to crave an explanation for this; and the answer to my inquiry was as nearly as possible in the following terms—'why, it is the Sunday School teachers. They must get their meat somewhere, and they gets it here".'[4] In a church in Radnorshire a visitor and his companion approached the communion rails and found the space within the sanctuary empty. The companion assured the visitor that there was indeed a Holy Table but that it might be in the schoolroom at the west end of the church, and there accordingly they found it behind a partition, placed for the master's use. The *Ecclesiologist* in 1841 reported that a new church at Lenton, two miles from Nottingham, had about a third of the chancel screened off as a vestry and that in the vestry a water-closet was about to be fixed actually contiguous to the altar itself.

Many churches, though, treated their Holy Tables with more respect, using them infrequently but keeping them decently, as the Church's canon law commanded. According to canon eighty-two, the Table was to be covered with 'a carpet of silk or other decent stuff' during the time of divine service, which entailed putting a covering over it at least on Sundays. The canon did not demand that such a covering should be permanent and, indeed, with the depredations of mice always a possibility—they ate the book-markers at Bettws chapel near Clyro—it might not be advisable to leave such a covering in church during the week, though no doubt some churches did. It was further ordered that, when the communion was administered, there should be also on the altar 'a fair linen cloth' and the parish was charged to see that the Ten Commandments were set up at the east end of the church, where the people could best see and read them, together with other sentences, which might be written on the walls. Behind the altar, then, parishioners most commonly would see the Ten Commandments, flanked by the Lord's Prayer and the Apostles' Creed, though the figures of Moses and Aaron might make their appearance and other embellishments might be introduced. A small canopy was placed over the altar in the church at Rode Hill, Somerset, built by Archdeacon Daubeny in 1824.

Not all incumbents conducted services in mediaeval churches for there had been some church building and rebuilding after the Reformation, as there was at Rode Hill. The new churches might be square, rectangular or elliptical, designed so that pulpit, reading-desk, clerk's seat and altar were grouped together at one focal point in order that all could see the minister and hear him, whether the service was morning or evening prayer or the communion. The vicars of Kings Norton in Leicestershire inherited a church rebuilt between 1760 and 1775 and throughout the nineteenth century conducted services in it from a three-decker pulpit placed centrally and facing west, so that they had their backs to the altar. When the sacrament was administered, the people, sitting in their pews on each side, looked past the pulpit to see the Holy Table. In other churches reading-desk and pulpit might be behind the altar and raised above it, as they were in the elliptical churches of St. Andrew's, Dublin, and All Saints, Newcastle-on-Tyne, early in the nineteenth century, so that their incumbents taking the usual Sunday services, looked over the altar towards the people in their pews. But the arrangement that came more and more to be favoured at that time was the separation of the reading-desk and pulpit and the placing of them, one on each side of the altar as at St. Philip's, Regent Street in London, built in 1820 as a chapel of ease to St. James's, Piccadilly. This lessened the visual domination of the pulpit and yet kept in the church the one focal point, for altar, pulpit and reading-desk remained grouped together.

St. Philip's, Regent Street, was a church built with the aid of a grant from the Church Building Commissioners, established to administer the Church Building Act of 1818. Given a parliamentary grant of a million pounds and charged with the duty of providing churches giving 'a proper accommodation for the largest number of persons at the least expense' in the rapidly expanding towns, where there was a dearth of churches, by 1821 they had built eight-five of them, had eighty thousand pounds remaining and twenty-five applications still in hand, which had to wait for lack of funds. A second grant of half a million was made in 1824, the result of an unexpected windfall from Austria which repaid a wartime loan that had been written off as lost, and gave the Commissioners a further lease of life. So large, cheap churches, holding up to two thousand people, appeared in the new suburbs and the old city centres, though since it was necessary that all inside them should be able to hear the ordinary human voice, this imposed a limit of some ninety feet in length and seventy in breadth and this in turn meant that galleries must be provided to accommodate such numbers in such a space. Consequently galleries were permitted, but square pews forbidden and other pews had to be low so all could see. The high churchmen on the Commission insisted that the altar should be properly regarded and therefore the east wall of the church was frequently recessed and the Holy Table stood there, with reading-desk on one side and pulpit on the other. Such large churches imposed a considerable strain upon their vicars, who found that they must bellow like bulls if they were to be heard. The Archbishop of York reported, 'I have lately made a circuit of the West Riding, and the reports that I have received from my clergy at different places convince me that smaller churches would here succeed better. In very few of the large ones, from the situation of the reading-desk and pulpit at the extremity of them, can the minister, unless gifted with a very powerful voice, make himself heard, and consequently the congregations are very thin.'[5] The rector of St. Andrew's, Holborn, pointed out that in large churches the strain on the voice was such that two ministers were required to do the duty and since it would be possible to pay for one only at the new church of St. Peter, Saffron Hill, it should be built to accommodate one thousand six hundred people rather than any more. But the Commissioners erected a church in Tudor Gothic on the hill, holding one thousand eight hundred, which was eventually demolished in 1955.

The churches the Commissioners built were cheap. They used cast iron as roofing, for window tracery, and in the columns of the nave arcade, while a bell turret might take the place of a tower, though it was recognised that a tower was desirable if the money could be had to build one. But even while these churches were going up, the clouds of a new movement were massing on the horizon, which were destined to change the whole religious scene and to influence virtually every incumbent and every church building in the land. The Oxford Movement may be fairly summarised in words that Pusey, one of its leaders and a saintly and learned professor at Christ Church, Oxford, used in 1840. The Tractarians who inspired the Movement, he wrote, paid high regard to baptism and communion; had a high estimate of episcopacy and of the visible Church; observed daily public prayers, fasts and feasts; had a regard for the visible part of devotion, such as the decoration of the house of God; and revered the ancient Church rather than the Reformation. The working out of these principles in churches was the task undertaken by two further groups of people. One was the Cambridge Camden Society, founded in 1839; the other was Dr. Hook, famous vicar of Leeds and his friend, Dr. John Jebb.

The Cambridge Camden Society, starting from the assumption that there was only one truly Christian style of architecture and that the style of the Middle Ages, advised the clergy and others what to do with their churches in the pages of the

Ecclesiologist. The finest flowering of Gothic, the Society maintained, was the Decorated style of the fourteenth century; earlier forms of Gothic, such as Norman, were primitive, and later forms of Gothic, like Perpendicular, were debased. New churches, therefore, should be Decorated and older churches should be remodelled if they did not conform to it; later accretions should be swept away. Inside the church the altar was to be honoured and was to stand within the chancel at its east end, for the ecclesiologists were convinced that every church should have a chancel. They believed, too, that it was from the chancel that the minister should conduct the services of morning and evening prayer and that this was the intention of the Prayer Book; therefore, the 'three decker' must be dismembered, the pulpit placed at one side of the nave at its east end, the reading-desk moved into the chancel and a lectern provided in the nave, opposite the pulpit, for the reading of the lessons.

Vicars proceeding to implement the promptings of the *Ecclesiologist* found that they must tread warily for the new arrangement entailed radical alterations to the pews, which hitherto had faced the pulpit in the nave but must now face east, a return to the Laudian ideal. Pews, however, could not be moved at the whim of the incumbent for parishioners might have rights in them. They might pay rent for the use of them and the rent was a valuable addition to parochial finances. At Sefton in Lancashire a pew belonged to a drinking and dining club founded by Liverpool merchants and gentlemen in 1771, who would drive out to Sefton on Sunday mornings, attend service, dine at the Punch Bowl Inn, where the attraction was Nellie Barker's cooking, attend evening prayer and drive home.[6] Pews might be attached to certain houses and when the houses changed hands, then the pews changed hands as well. Some of the clergy were hot against pews. J. M. Neale, a leading ecclesiologist, was an implacable enemy of them, attacked them with an axe when he went to Crawley in Sussex and poured derision on them whenever he could. The squire at Tong church, he reported in 1842, 'has built a pew in the Chancel; when the Commandments are begun, a servant regularly enters at the Chancel door with a luncheon tray'. R. S. Hawker demolished a pew in the nave of Morwenstow church while its owner stood by in amazement. But it was dangerous to act so high-handedly as John Allen, vicar of Prees in Lancashire and made Archdeacon of Salop in 1847, discovered when he tore off with his own hands the padlock of a pew belonging to a squire and found that the squire had a faculty for the same. The archdeacon had to confess his fault. Others proceeded more cautiously, gradually winning assent to these new ideas, like the vicar of Dunchurch who reported that the abolition of square pews in his church had been kindly consented to, and that Lord John Scott, the lay rector, had provided the pews in the chancel, keeping one only for himself and allowing the front rows to be filled by labouring men, who also occupied the steps in front of the communion rails.

The abolition of square pews and the lowering of the walls of all others and turning them east were made easier by other factors which helped towards these ends. The new pews might still be rented, as the old ones were, though a movement was on foot to make them free. The new arrangement also allowed more people to be accommodated in the church, for it was estimated that the substitution of open seats allowed for an increase of between twenty and fifty per cent in the number of kneelings, a valuable point since space was at a premium in the Victorian church which was now often full with worshippers. And then, again, the old reason for high pews, that they kept off the icy draughts, was no longer valid as technology advanced and the heating of churches became more effective. The first experiments in this field were not, indeed, greatly successful, as first experiments rarely are. At Dunchurch a stove, placed in the central passage, had as an appendage plentiful black piping which meandered about the church before making its exit. The sexton fed and raked this fiery monster all the time of the service as it alternately smoked and scorched the faithful so that it was abolished in favour of two Arnot stoves, in opposite corners of the church, but these, having no proper flues, proved to be a source of constant cost and annoyance. These, too, were removed and the purchase of a stove from Leamington at a cost of fourteen pounds was found to answer all requisite purposes. It was kept alight all the winter for an annual outlay of four pounds and fed daily every morning and evening with coke.[7]

If the old pews looked like large, lidless boxes and reminded J. C. Hare, rector of Hurstmonceux and Archdeacon of Lewes, of Smithfield Market, the new seats, arranged in regular rows gave the congregation the air of an army assembled for review. The Victorian congregation was more disciplined, probably more devout, than its Hanoverian predecessor. The privacy of the high pew had gone and worshippers, instead of looking at the wainscoting of their pews and their vicar high above them in the reading-desk and pulpit, looked at the backs of the people in the seats in front of them and at their vicar in the chancel beyond. Keble designed the pews at Hursley so that it was nearly impossible when in them to assume an attitude that was not really devotional. The allocation of these new seats, however, could prove a delicate matter. It was the duty of the churchwardens, not the incumbent, to seat the parishioners but they found this sometimes such an unpleasant task, giving rise to animosities within the parish, that they might ask a few of the neighbouring clergy to do this for them, or even the archdeacon. Nevertheless, it was the duty of the churchwardens to assign seats to the parishioners according to their rank and station so that the re-arrangement of their church might cause them considerable concern.

Sunday services in the early nineteenth century were enlivened by a choir which might occupy a gallery at the west end of the church and be accompanied in its singing by a few instrumentalists, all wearing their usual Sunday clothes. John Byng, later Viscount Torrington, reporting on the singers that he encounted on his travels, came to Folkingham in Lincolnshire in the summer of 1791, found an enormous market square and a late Perpendicular tower at the church and discovered, inside, 'a singing-loft crowded; and amongst them one lady in a blue silk bonnet, who sung notably, but the bas-

soons and hautboys were too loud and shrieking'. Much later
Thomas Hardy described in *The Mayor of Casterbridge* how,
on a Sunday afternoon when service was over, a large con-
tingent of church-goers filed across from the church to the
Three Mariners, the rear of this procession being formed by
the choir with their bass-viols, fiddles and flutes under their
arms. They sat down to half-a-pint of liquor, no more, discussed the sermon and might sing the metrical version of a
psalm. The choir was a powerful and influential body of
organised opinion in the parish and an incumbent had to treat
it carefully. As a result of the arrival of the recently married
daughter of the Lady of the Manor at Camerton in 1822, the
singers there were in a perpetual state of intoxication so that
on Sunday, July 14th at evening church the rector refused to
let them chant the service after the first lesson, whereupon
some dozen or more of them picked up their hats and left the
building. The service continued and later the rector recorded
the event in verse:

> Some merry musicians quite fresh from the barrel
> Last Sunday resolved with Religion to quarrel,
> So, quitting their seats in the midst of the prayers,
> Clapp'd their hats on their noddles and hurried down-
> stairs—
> Conceiving by thus turning backs on the Church
> Both Parson and People were left in the lurch.
> But Parson and People had a more serious thing
> To attend to than hear these blythe revellers sing,
> The subject was Death! for only three days before
> To the grave, where vain mortals can revel no more,
> A companion was borne, once as healthy and strong
> As themselves, who now trip it so joyous along.

The rector, therefore, asked the question:

> Of these short-lived carousers reflection may ask,
> Is it wisdom to barter their souls for a cask?[8]

But choirs were soon to be removed from their galleries and would no longer be able to hurry downstairs, for in the 1840s F. W. Hook at Leeds was experimenting with an idea that was to revolutionise the singing in parish churches, sending choirs into chancels. At Leeds, Hook pulled down the old church and built a new one, of no great architectural merit, seating nearly three thousand. In this church, the nave as before, was for the congregation; and the clergy, as the ecclesiologists demanded, were put into the chancel with the altar at its east end; but now came the innovation, for the clergy were joined in the chancel by a surpliced choir. A surpliced choir was not new at Leeds, for cassocks and surplices were introduced for the singers there as early as 1818, perhaps the first instance in a parish church in England of such a thing; but its position was a novelty and due mainly to the ideas of Hook and his friend, John Jebb. Jebb thought that the worship of the Church of England was best seen in the sung daily service of her cathedrals and that 'her white-robed companies of men and boys, stationed at each side of her chancels, midway between the porch and the altar' was the nearest possible approach to a primitive and heavenly pattern. He did not, however, like the choir sitting among the congregation, as in cathedrals, and advocated a position between the congregation and the altar. At the time of the consecration of the new church it was explained that the surplices of the choir showed that it was to be its sacred duty to help the clergy in leading public worship; and that, because of this, it was placed nearer the altar than the laity.

The clergy looked at Leeds and then looked at their own churches, wondered whether they might not put their choirs into the chancel and, having wondered a little, began to move them there from their galleries. Since Leeds was an exception in having a surpliced choir already, and the usual church choir was unrobed, choirs making their first appearance in the chancel were not at first robed in surplices either: that followed after the new arrangement was well established and the parish had accepted it. The resulting effect of surpliced singers sitting near the altar, with the vicar among them, could be pleasing, reminding worshippers of angels round the heavenly throne when seen from a distance; and where the choir was good and well disciplined and the chancel was spacious, there was much to be said for the change and certainly it proved popular. It was not so satisfactory, however, where the choir was poor and ill-disciplined and crammed into a narrow chancel, obstructing the view of the altar and distracting the congregation with its behaviour. The choir needed firm handling. Canon Newbolt of St. Paul's, who gave advice to the clergy in several books at the end of the nineteenth century, asserted this frequently. The choir might have two standards of excellence, religious and musical, fail conspicuously in both and have no money. The boys of the choir should be treated with a firm discipline. 'Difficult, disappointing, distracting folk are choirs,' he observed, and to be in charge of one requires 'a great deal of prayer, watchfulness and inflexible severity'.[9]

Choirs were not moved into chancels without protest, however, and some asked whether they were necessary in a parish at all. That extreme conservative, J. W. Burgon, queried the copying of cathedral services in a parish and demanded dramatically, 'who, in his senses, would exchange the rough melody of five hundred lusty voices, singing with all their hearts to God . . . for the scientific screeching of a score of little boys and girls in the chancel, or the pretentious cadences of half-a-dozen men and women in the gallery?' Bishop Blomfield thought that surpliced choirs walking in procession in parish churches were not desirable, and sometimes, when the singers first appeared in all the glory of their white and billowing folds, they were derided as whitewashed saints. Some parishes never followed the fashion, either because they were content with the old ways or because they were too small to do so. Flora Thompson recalled her tiny church on the Oxfordshire-Northamptonshire border about 1880 where there was no surpliced choir but instead;

the squire's and clergyman's families had pews in the chancel, with backs to the wall on either side, and between them stood two long benches for the schoolchildren, well under the eye of authority. Below the steps down into the nave stood the harmonium, played by the clergyman's daughter, and round it was ranged the choir of small schoolgirls. Then came the rank and file of the congregation, nicely graded, with the farmer's family in the front row, then the Squire's gardener and coachman, the schoolmistress, the maid-servants, and the cottages, with the Parish Clerk at the back to keep order.[10]

The harmonium mentioned by Flora Thompson is a reminder of another musical change that came to the churches, for the old church bands were dissolved, the fiddles and flutes heard no more, and harmoniums, barrel-organs and organs proper took their place. There was an harmonium in the church at Chilcombe in Dorset in 1874, which was played by the rector while the parish clerk sang, but then there were only twenty people in the place. Barrel-organs had a limited repertoire and were frowned upon by musicians like Ouseley, who compared them to an oriental prayer-wheel, but they were popular and one had appeared as early as the 1820s in the church at Ampton in Suffolk, where it was placed in the gallery and which it was the duty of Lord Calthorpe's butler to grind. At Jevington in Sussex a barrel-organ was over-hastily installed in the church, wound up and duly played a psalm for Sunday worship, but then proceeded to 'Drops of Brandy' and 'Go to the devil and shake yourself' before it was carried out into the churchyard where by degrees it played itself out. Slowly, harmoniums and barrel-organs gave way to organs; at Berwick in Sussex an harmonium was introduced in 1862, an organ in 1880. They were not always introduced without opposition and the clergy had to go carefully, as the rector did at Pluckley in Kent when the squire's wife gave a London-made organ to the church. Wisely, he invited everyone, including the choir, to sign an address of thanks for the gift, which bound them to the use of the instrument and meant that the choir must move from the gallery to a place in the chancel where the new organ was installed. So these large, cumbersome, versatile machines became the usual accompaniment to later Victorian worship, though a few voices were raised complaining that they were becoming too noisy, too obtrusive and too big.

When the vicar went to the altar to celebrate the communion he would, in the earlier years of the nineteenth century, move to the north side as the Prayer Book ordered, a direction made, it seems, when the Holy Table might be placed in the middle of the chancel or the nave, with its ends east and west. In 1800 the Table was set altarwise and the priest went to the north and shorter side. The Tractarians observed this custom; Newman at St. Mary's, Oxford, and Pusey at the cathedral there celebrated at the north end, and a parishioner at Whatley, R. W. Church's parish in Somerset, recalled how they were all impressed by 'the extreme solemnity and devotion with which Mr. Church celebrated the Holy Communion. We had heard nothing then about the Eastward position, but I can see now his slight figure bending in lowly reverence before the altar, giving the whole service a new and higher and holier meaning by his bearing and entire absorption in the act of worship'. The evangelical clergy stood in the same position as the Tractarians and continued to stand there throughout the century, but later generations of clergy influenced by the Oxford Movement moved round to the west side of the altar and faced east, thinking that it gave greater honour to the sacrament to do so, that it emphasised the role of the priest as leader of the worship of the congregation and that it was the position in which the priests of mediaeval England stood. A high regard for the sacrament led to other innovations also, the wearing of the eucharistic vestments, the lighting of candles on the altar, the placing of a cross and flowers on it and the hanging of coloured frontals before it, so that some churches began to take on a distinctly catholic appearance which would have made them not unacceptable in Rome. Against this tide of ritualism and decoration the bishops and the law fulminated largely in vain, for, like Canute, their admonitions were incapable of halting its advancing waves. Bishop Phillpotts attended St. John's

Church, Torquay, on Easter Day, 1847, and found there on the Communion Table two patens, four chalices, a flagon, alms dish, silver spoon and large alms chest, all normal. He found also a wooden cross decorated with flowers and evergreens and two small glass flower vases. Seizing one of the vases, he pushed if off the altar; but, finding it dangling, with water and flowers strewing the floor, realised that it was attached to the Holy Table by a string. He left the other vase alone. It was an incident in a way symbolic of episcopal helplessness in the face of determined parish priests.

The law was equally helpless in the face of the ritualists for the law was obscure, its decisions contradictory, its authority questioned and its punishments ineffective. 'Was it lawful to stand at the altar facing east?' the law was asked. The Judicial Committee of the Privy Council declared that it was not, in the Purchas Judgment of 1871, though two canons of St. Paul's stood in that position when they celebrated the communion. Yet six years later in the Ridsdale Judgment it authorised the Eastward position, provided that the manual acts of the celebrant were visible to the congregation. Ridsdale was the vicar of St. Peter's, a church high on the cliffs of Folkestone looking down on its harbour, with a liking for the Stations of the Cross and other aids to devotion more acceptable across the Channel. Ten judges and five assessors condemned some of his practices. The law took four years over his case, but he remained in his parish fifty-five years and served there under four Archbishops of Canterbury, none of whom could dislodge him, until he resigned in 1923. Father MacKonochie, vicar of St. Alban's, Holborn, was also condemned by the Judicial Committee of the privy Council for his anglo-catholic practices and was prepared to acknowledge its decision even if he found ways of avoiding its severities. If he were not allowed to elevate the paten above his head, then he would elevate it to his chin; if he could not prostrate himself before the altar, then he could genuflect; if he could not genuflect, then he could bow; and if there were to be no lighted candles on the altar, then he would have seven lamps above it. Suspended in 1875, he went on holiday to Italy.

Archbishop Tait persuaded him some years later to resign his benefice and he died, lost on the moors in Scotland, in 1887, but not before he had seen the full splendour of High Mass restored to St. Alban's in 1884.[11] The Public Worship Regulation Act of 1874 endeavoured to give teeth to the law when it proceeded against the ritualists and as a result five clergymen were imprisoned for contempt of court. But the Act was ineffective. The Rev. Arthur Tooth was presented to the living of Hatcham in the same year that Ridsdale went to Folkestone. He refused to alter the services in his church and went to prison for twenty-eight days in 1877. On his release he found his church locked against him but, with the help of a small boy, squeezed through a small window and resumed his ministry. So neither the law nor the bishops could alter the fact that the anglo-catholics had come to stay. In 1900, therefore, incumbents officiated in many more ways than they had done so a hundred years before. At one extreme there was morning prayer and sermon, simple and austere, with the clergyman in a surplice for morning prayer and in a gown for the sermon; and at the other there was High Mass, with incense, candles, vestments, and the Eastward position. Most incumbents conducted services that came somewhere in between.

Most incumbents, too, used the *Book of Common Prayer*, which was regarded universally as one of the chief glories of the Church, though it involved two hours' worship on a Sunday morning and in the afternoon perhaps an hour and a half. Bishops were accustomed to tell their clergy that the whole service of the Prayer Book should be used on Sundays and read with a distinct and audible voice; Bishop Mant of Down and Connor assured the clergy of his diocese, 'it is one of the greatest blessings conferred upon us, as members of the Protestant Church of England and Ireland, that we are provided with the most admirable forms of supplicating God in a language which we understand'. The evangelicals were content with it; the Tractarians defended it; and Burgon suggested that anyone who found the use of it a hardship, laid himself open to the gravest suspicion that he was unsound in the faith.

Keble defended the length of the service and blamed weak faith, careless men and the vanities of the world if they seemed too long:

'But Faith is cold, and wilful men are strong,
And the blithe world, with bells and harness proud,
Rides tinkling by, so musical and loud,
It drowns the eternal word, the angelic song;
And one by one the weary listless throng
Steals out of church, and leaves the choir unseen
Of winged Guards to weep, where prayer had been,
That souls immortal find that hour too long.

Nevertheless, some brave liberal voices began to be heard saying that the Prayer Book was not perfect, that the Athanasian Creed with its damnatory clauses might be omitted from it with profit, that the Sunday morning service was too long and might be abridged, that the lectionary needed revision, and that the catechism, the marriage service and the service for the burial of the dead required modification. But they were voices for a long time crying in the wilderness and the first official change in the Prayer Book, when it came in 1859, was hardly epoch-making, entailing merely the removal of the three special services for Charles I King and Martyr, the birth and restoration of Charles II, and that which celebrated the deliverance from the Papist conspiracy on November 5th.[12]

Then, in 1870, a new scheme for the reading of the Bible in the services was approved; many passages were shortened, chapter divisions were disregarded where continuity demanded it, and some old lessons dropped while some new ones were added. Conservatives did not like the changes and Burgon revenged himself on the new and shorter lessons by reading them monstrous slow. Bishop Christopher Wordsworth of Lincoln was critical, also, and regretted 'the scanty pittance of the Word of Life which is now doled out to our congregations, especially on the Lord's Day'. He thought, too, that it was squeamish and noted that it omitted the story in Genesis of Jacob's daughter, Dinah, who was taken to bed by the uncircumcised son of the local prince, which led to retribution at the hands of Dinah's brothers, who killed both the prince and his son. It was a warning, the bishop thought, needed in rural villages as well as cities, and one on which the clergy ought to preach.

More important than the revision of the lectionary was the Act of Uniformity Amendment Act of 1872, which, though it did not release the clergy from the Prayer Book, allowed the adaptation of its services for special needs. The Act allowed the clergy to make, on special occasions, their own selection of material from the Bible and the Prayer Book, if the bishop agreed; and sermons could now be delivered apart from divine service, provided that they were accompanied by Prayer Book prayers. But, more than this, it sliced like a knife into the traditional structure of the Sunday morning service, dividing it into its three parts and allowing matins, the litany and the communion to be used separately. Now it was possible to have matins alone, or the communion alone, or to transfer the litany to evening prayer, with the result that the main Sunday morning service could be much shorter and accommodated within an hour, to the relief of many vicars and congregations. The practice was adopted in many places of having the communion every Sunday at eight a.m. and of making morning prayer, held later, the main Sunday morning service. Perhaps it encouraged laziness. It certainly led to greater diversity, but abbreviation was required.

If the Bible and the Prayer Book were the substance of the worship of the Church, the hymns were its icing. At the beginning of the nineteenth century, Anglican churches sang the psalms in a metrical version, either old or new, and there were collections of hymns which existed alongside of them. 'While shepherds watched their flocks by night' had appeared in such a supplement in 1700 and a multiplicity of private hymn-books were in use in churches in the eighteenth century. Hymns, however, were frowned on in the Church of England by both high churchmen and evangelicals, were called 'the meretricious trappings of the conventicle' by

Bishop Mant, and regarded as the preserve of the more effer-
vescent Methodists and Independents. Keble wrote *The
Christian Year*, and in it 'Sun of my soul, thou Saviour dear',
not to be sung in church but said at the bedside. Such a popular form of devotion, however, could not be forbidden for
ever, and in the nineteenth century hymn-singing swept into
all the churches, with *Hymns Ancient and Modern*, first published in 1860 and 1861, on the crest of the wave. *Hymns
Ancient and Modern* succeeded in meeting the needs of parish
churches as no other hymn-book did, providing both words
and music that congregations liked to sing. The first edition
contained 'Abide with me', written by H. F. Lyte at Brixham
and published in leaflet form in 1847, printed with its famous
tune composed by W. H. Monk, though Lyte had written for it
a different melody. The practice of issuing supplements and
the making of a revised edition in 1875 ensured that it kept
pace with changing needs and allowed it, for example, first to
incorporate 'Onward, Christian soldiers', which had been
written by Baring-Gould for the Sunday school children of
Horbury Brig in 1864, and then, later, to match it with the
well-known tune by Arthur Sullivan. Hymns had come to
stay; Liddon believed that they did more than anything to
keep religion alive among the masses.

Evening prayer was generally held in the afternoon, though
in the towns after about 1830 it was more likely to be in the
evening and some churches held both afternoon and evening
services if they attracted large congregations. Hook at Holy
Trinity, Coventry, began Sunday evening services in the
summer of 1830 and nearly two thousand came to them. The
vestry, therefore, asked for the services to be continued, so
the church was lit by gas in November of that year and evening services were held throughout the winter, making it the
first church in Coventry to do this. In the towns the evening
service proved to be more popular than the afternoon, for the
census of 1851 showed that of those attending Anglican worship in the churches of Sheffield on Sunday, March 30th of
that year, six thousand two hundred and ninety-one went in
the morning, two thousand nine hundred and thirty-four in

the afternoon and five thousand six hundred and fifty-six in the evening. The parish of Whitechapel, London, had a population of thirty six thousand and a famous evangelical vicar in W. W. Champneys; his church was reported in the same census to have attracted 1,547 in the morning, 827 in the afternoon and 1,642 in the evening, so the proportions were not far different from those at Sheffield. Evangelical churches might have communion in the afternoon or evening. The rector of Birmingham began an afternoon communion in 1851 and thirty years later the Bishop of Rochester found that a hundred out of his 291 parishes had communion in the evening. High churchmen did not regard this with favour.

The Prayer Book directed that after the second lesson at evening prayer, the children of the parish should be examined in the catechism and Bishop Otter of Chichester thought it to be an unpleasant but necessary task. Some incumbents found it useful, both for the children and for the adults who listened, though it had its dangers for the children's unexpected answers might make the congregation rock with laughter. E. B. Ellman tried it at Berwick in Sussex but gave up the practice when he found the children nervous and that one boy said: 'I renounce the pomps and vanities of the Christian Faith!' Henry Mansel, a famous teacher at Oxford, at the age of three insisted in standing up and saying the catechism with the rest at Cosgrove, where his father was rector. When asked by his father how many commandments there were, he replied, 'Ten,' immediately adding, to the discomfiture of his parent, 'Which be they?' At St. Mary's, Oxford, Burgon explained to his boys how David took five stones in his scrip with which to slay Goliath and how these represented the books of the Pentateuch, from one book of which, Deuteronomy, Jesus in his temptation in the wilderness took passages with which to defeat the Tempter. When asked why David took five stones, a boy suggested that there were more giants; 'mayhap'e thowt there must be some more on 'em about'. The boy, rather than Burgon, might today be thought nearer the mark. At Hursley, Keble catechised the boys one Sunday and the girls the next, and sometimes catechising was found to be useful as an extension of Sunday school where the Sunday school was big. At Leeds, Hook had the first classes of his Sunday schools brought to him at the conclusion of the afternoon service, when he made them say the catechism and questioned them, ending with a short address. Catechising was found useful for the children of the upper classes, who would never go to Sunday school but would attend afternoon service. Some of these children were very ignorant, Canon Miller of Rochester complained.[13] Lang catechised over fifteen hundred children on his first Sunday at Portsea.

One of the best examples of the art of catechising in the nineteenth century, however, comes not from England but from France where one day in 1855 Samuel Wilberforce came across a catechism class in the Lady Chapel at St. Ouen and found it instructive.

'The Abbé was perfectly familiar, making them laugh freely and then gathering them up into seriousness, and so keeping the attention of their young minds through a good hour. Q. 'What is God?' 'A Spirit.' 'Can you see a spirit?' 'Have you a spirit—what is it?' 'My soul.' 'Come now, Mademoiselle B: you are a savant, did you ever see your soul?' 'No.' 'What, never?' 'Are you sure?' . . . etc. 'Then why, if God is a Spirit, and cannot be seen, is He painted as a very old man with hair so white and so white a beard?' No answer. 'It is a representation, my children, to teach you, not that God has a form like an old man, but that He has perfectly all that old men are supposed to have. An old man has lived long. God has lived for ever. An old man has wisdom, judgment. God is all wise. The Judge, *voyons*. God is perfection. Now, what is perfection?' A pause; and then a girl said, 'When a thing is *bien fait*.' With both hands up, and an air of wonder, the Priest, '*Bien fait, bien fait.* Can anyone say better?'[14]

Before children could be catechised, however, they must be baptised and made members of the Church; and for that sacrament water was needed and a font. Fonts were generally by the door 'to signify entrance into God's church by baptism' and to prevent the font being moved elsewhere bishops liked to insist on the canon law that it should be of stone; but though it was symbolically useful to place it at the west end of the church, it was inconvenient if baptisms took place after the second lesson at morning or evening prayer, for then the congregation could see little of what took place. Some churches, therefore, had the font by the altar. The font at St. George's, Hanover Square, London, the *Ecclesiologist* reported, was like a tolerably sized marble wine-cooler, fixed in a circular oak frame about a foot high, which was kept under the altar and could be wheeled out, since it was on castors, when required; and it was common in Ireland to put a bason on the altar when baptisms were to be performed. Some churches had not fonts. When Bishop Phillpotts visited the Scilly Isles in 1831 he found that the church at Hugh Town on St. Mary's did not have one and Walsham How reported that three churches in the rural deanery of Oswestry were without them; no doubt they used basons also for the administration of the sacrament. Fonts, if they existed, were not always used, nor treated with reverence, for they might be receptacles for odd candle ends and, if they happened to be in that part of the church where a school was held, might be filled with slates and fragments of books. The vicar of Fordington in Dorset told Francis Kilvert in 1874 that when he had come to his parish nearly half a century before he found that no man had ever been known to receive the communion except the parson, the clerk and the sexton; and once, when he was to hold a christening, he found there was no water in the font. 'Water, sir!' said the clerk in astonishment. 'The last parson never used no water. He spit into his hand.' One young clergyman boasted that the children he baptised never cried because he never let the water touch them; and when there was water, there might be ice in the font in the winter. The rector of Litlington in Sussex did not baptise his children individually as they were born but baptised them in batches, two or three at a time.

The clergy faced several problems in baptism, one of which

was the difficulty, known in all ages, of conducting the service with dignity if the children howled continually during the proceedings. In the country, where a child or two was the most that usually came forward for a baptism, the problem was not severe, though Burgon reported how, when he baptised at West Ilsley on the Berkshire Downs before a full congregation, one of the children bawled at the top of her lungs, 'Give me my bonnet, I say, and let me go ho-o-oo-me.' But in large parishes, with many infants being brought to church for baptism, the result must sometimes have been pandemonium. When Maclagan went to St. Mary's, Newington, London in 1869 he baptised fifty children on his first Easter afternoon and thirty adults in the evening, though this was exceptional for the parish had been greatly neglected. The sheer numbers of those brought to baptism could exhaust the clergy, as it must have done at Leeds where, before Hook's arrival, the previous vicar and two curates baptised twice every day and so in a year baptised nearly two thousand. Then there was the difficulty of godparents, who might have little or no idea of what they were promising at the font. At Camerton John Skinner baptised during the evening service on Easter Day, 1830, and was sure that neither of the godfathers had any idea of the promises that they had to make. At the end of the century it was still a difficulty that godparents were not sufficiently instructed in their responsibilites, though E. S. Talbot gathered from the clergy of his diocese of Rochester in 1899 that they preferred to baptise even if there was a want of sponsors, and he thought that they were right.[15] Parents who wished to give unsuitable names, like Nero, to their children, was another problem that the clergy encountered; and there was the problem, too, of the very poor parents who felt that they could not decently bring their child to church because of the rags in which it must be clothed. But Flora Thompson remembered how in her parish the clergyman's daughter kept two christening robes which could be lent to mothers and this was common practice in the country.

There was much discussion in the first half of the century concerning the effect of baptism on the infants which were brought to the font and there made members of the Church. After a child had been baptised, having been dipped in the water discreetly and warily or, more commonly, had water poured upon him (for so the Prayer Book ordered), and having been signed with the sign of the cross, the priest then declared the child to be regenerate. But how was the child regenerate? The debate came to a head when Bishop Phillpotts refused to institute the Rev. G. C. Gorham to the living of Brampford Speke because he thought that Mr. Gorham's views on baptismal regeneration were not those of the Church of England. It was a cloudy subject, and as men looked into its depths they were not sure what they could see, for Gorham maintained that regeneration was not always given to infants in baptism, though it might be so given, while the bishop rested his case on the Prayer Book and argued that children baptised were unconditionally regenerate. The case was argued furiously between the bishop and Mr. Gorham; and it was argued no less furiously in the courts, from which Gorham emerged victorious and was duly instituted to his living. The case led to secessions to the Church of Rome, for the State had ruled that Gorham's views were permissible within the Church and had ruled, therefore, upon a point of doctrine. But the controversy over baptismal regeneration had exhausted itself and did not again rouse passions in the Church. The laity continued to regard baptism as important, whatever its effect might be, and, indeed, proved to have an increasing appetite for it, since by 1900 the Anglican clergy were baptising a higher percentage of the population, both absolutely and relatively, than they had before. In 1885 they had baptised 623 in each thousand live births; in 1895, 641 per thousand; and in 1902, 658 per thousand.

Keble enjoyed taking baptisms but was melancholy at weddings. 'A village wedding,' he wrote to Miss Hicks Beach, 'is in general the most melancholy of all ceremonies to me,' and the reason for his sadness was the usual pregnancy of the bride who came to the altar. When J. C. Hare gave a charge to the clergy of the Archdeaconry of Lewes in 1841 he reported that in his own parish of Hurstmonceux—and in others, too, so he had heard—numbers of brides from among the lower orders were wont to come to be married 'with the offspring of unhallowed lust lying beneath their bosoms!' and thought that the Church must speak out on this. It was not, however, the only reason why the clergy found it unpleasant to solemnise matrimony, for it could be that one or other or both of the parties to be married might be drunk. A Liverpool clergyman pointed out that the sign of a cross in a marriage register was not necessarily the sign of a lack of education, for in his experience, in one case out of five, one of the parties could not sign their name because drink had incapacitated them from doing so.[16] Some clergy developed an antipathy to the marriage service. Patrick Brontë had ceased taking it before Charlotte was married, leaving the duty to the curate; and though Charlotte's marriage to Arthur Nicholls on June 29th, 1854, was a decorous affair at eight in the morning, he refused to attend, though he was very cheerful at the wedding breakfast after.

Till 1837 Anglican clergymen were responsible for all marriages in England and Wales, with the exception of those made by Quakers and by Jews; and since marriage was a legal ceremony as well as a religious one, their registers were of importance to the State. They were not always well kept, might lie around in damp, unheated churches or be carried off to the parsonage or a churchwarden's house and so mislaid; therefore an Act of 1812 ordered churches to keep their registers in an iron chest to be bought at the expense of the parish, so that today many vestries contain chests of about that date. Clergymen were not always efficient registrars and as late as 1888 complaints were still being made that some registers were nearly illegible. Then, in 1836, two Acts were passed which allowed marriage in a dissenting chapel or before a registrar and which required Anglican clergy, who were still to act as registrars in their own churches, to send copies of their registers to an official designated for that purpose. Incumbents did not object so much to the new freedom granted by the Marriage Act, for it meant that they need no longer marry dissenters or freethinkers, as to the new instructions for registration, which they regarded as vexatious. They continued to marry the greater proportion of the population but slowly their percentage fell and, for every thousand marriages in England and in Wales, their proportion dropped from nine hundred and seven in 1844 to six hundred and eighty-six fifty years later, while Roman Catholic marriages, nonconformist marriages, Jewish marriages and civil marriages crept up.

In 1800 the clergy were not anxious about divorce, for the law did not allow it except to those wealthy and influential enough to obtain it by Act of Parliament and these were few. By the middle of the century, however, Members of Parliament were demanding that it should be easier to obtain, which raised problems for the clergy, for the clergy were against divorce. What would happen, it was asked, if, after a divorce, a man presented himself at his parish church and demanded to be remarried there? And would the vicar, who perhaps believed that God had forbidden remarriage, be compelled to take the service? In 1857 the law settled the problem by allowing a clergyman to refuse to marry a guilty party in his church but ordering him to allow its use for such a purpose to any clergyman of the same diocese who was prepared to take the wedding; but the clergy did not often have to allow this in the nineteenth century, for the number of divorces remained small and there were not many more than six hundred of them in 1901.

Some churches had bells, enough to ring at a wedding, and where there were bells there were bellringers whom the clergy were advised to visit when they rang on special occasions. One writer advised the clergy that chiming was better than ringing, since ringing could be dangerous to the fabric, required great exertion and generated thirst.

Outside the services authorised in the Prayer Book, some incumbents experimented with a children's service in church at which adults were not present. The vicar of Dunchurch would spend an hour at the communion rails with the children of wealthier parents and younger members of his own family, and afterwards catechise them with others on holy days and the last Sunday of the month. When St. Agatha's mission at Portsmouth was opened in 1884 the children's service was held in the Holy Trinity Church on Sunday afternoon; but the behaviour of the larger boys was so bad that the vicar left the chancel saying to the mission priest, 'I leave my church to you and your savage crew.' The children's service was transferred to the mission church but Dolling, who came in the succeeding year, found that the conduct of the children had not improved and described how;

> two boys calmly lighted their pipes and began to smoke. One remedy alone seemed possible—to seize them by the back of the neck and run them out of church, knocking their heads together as hard as I could. Amazed at first into silence, their tongues recovered themselves before they reached the door, and the rest of the children listened, delighted, to vocabulary which I have seldom heard excelled. We had no sooner restored order than the mothers of the two lads put in an appearance. As wine is to water, so was the conversation of the mothers to the sons. I wish I could have closed the children's ears as quickly as I closed the service. But they listened with extreme delight, even following me in a kind of procession, headed by the two ladies, to my lodgings.[17]

Much quieter and less eventful were the weekday services of morning and evening prayer, which the Tractarians especially enjoyed saying in their churches. Keble, not surprisingly, was a great advocate of these and sometimes they were surprisingly well attended. Armstrong at East Dereham began them in his church in 1853 and was gratified to find on the first day, February 10th, that forty-two were present, though there was snow on the ground, while a month later eighty came. But even if only two or three came they could console themselves with the thought that angels and archangels were worshipping with them and that the 'solemn dead' as Isaac Williams called them, whose bones lay in the vaults beneath their feet and out in the churchyard, were in a sense also present.

If there were few worshippers in the week, however, there were many on Sunday and most incumbents then expected full churches or, if they were not full, at least large congregations so that the Sunday services were important occasions. George Eliot pictured, in *Janet's Repentance*, a Sunday morning service at Milby church which she was inclined to think was, for the younger ladies and gentlemen of the parish, the most exciting event of the week; few places could present a more brilliant show of outdoor toilettes than might be seen issuing from the church there at one o'clock on a Sunday. The behaviour of those within might not be all that could be desired, for there was considerable levity during the prayers and the sermon, but at least the people were present and if there had been a good resident incumbent rather than an old curate whose wig was nearly always awry, there might have been more decorum. Vicars and rectors looked out on a sea of faces when they led divine worship, felt the excitement of a well-filled building and had the sensation that they were supported by a large body of the faithful and the not-so-faithful. At St. Paul's, Sheffield, in the centre of the town, there were eight hundred present at the morning service and twelve hundred at night, many of them men, and the congregation was not attracted, it was suggested, by 'sensational services, midnight missions, or religious novelties, home or imported'. A census in Sheffield in 1881 showed that Anglican churches attracted congregations of two or three hundred at the least and that three of them had evening congregations of over a thousand. Nor was the large congregation restricted to the town, for village churches were full of villagers, as at Berwick, Sussex, where a population of one hundred and seventy produced average attendances in the winter of eighty-one on a Sunday morning and ninety in the afternoon.

But still there were the unchurched masses. Francis Kilvert encountered an old man in 1874 and had an interesting conversation. 'Leaning over a cottage garden gate I found an old man with a tall black hat, shiny brown leather leggings, and a cunning eye. He pointed out to me the way to Ford. I asked him where he went to Church. Screwing up his crafty eye he fixed the other on me. "Anywheres" he said, vaguely. Alas, I knew that "Anywheres"meant "Nowheres". "This here bottom," he continued in an explanatory and condescending tone, "this here bottom's a place by itself. It belongs to Church Gatton, but there ain't no worship here." ' For many did not go to church. A census of certain cities in 1881 found that nearly thirty-eight per cent of their population attended church or chapel on a Sunday; if the proportion in the countryside were higher, then perhaps almost half the people were going to Sunday worship. But the other half did not and though it was possible to forget this, it was not possible to forget it all the time, for here was a problem that would not go away. Vicars of churches in certain areas, confronted on Sundays with rows of empty pews, could not forget it and their bishops could not forget it, and both wondered what to do.

In 1839 Bethnal Green had a population of seventy thousand and two churches. A great flurry of building in the next eleven years produced ten new ones, each named after one of the apostles, like St. Thomas's, with its schools and parsonage, built on the site of the Nova Scotia Gardens, which was notorious as the haunt of those who procured subjects for dissection by secret assassination. The new schools were crowded but the new churches were not and Bishop Blomfield was forced to recognise that in that area there was a missionary situation, for though the people became more friendly to the Church this did not lead them to embrace its worship. For the incumbents of such areas the work was tough. The vicar of St. Andrew's, Bethnal Green, lamented in 1858, 'my position is productive of what I might venture to call mental torture' and the priest-in-charge of St. Peter's, Hackney Road, recommended a more frequent change of incumbents, though his own vicar was Bishop Beckles of Sierra Leone and lived in Eastbourne in 1883.[18] Fifteen years later the bishop was still the vicar and still non-resident. Nor did the splendour of anglo-catholic ritual always appeal to the working classes, even if there were some great successes in anglo-catholic parishes. All Saints, Lambeth, stood in the middle of a market like Petticoat Lane, with gin palaces, beer shops and decayed vegetation washing round it walls. The church could seat two thousand, had an altar in an apse, a blue dome showered with golden stars, a good organ and Gregorian chants; but there were not quite a dozen at High Mass, though there were more in the evening when the poor and the friends of the choir came.

The increasing mobility of the population, brought about by the railway and the bicycle, lessened to some extent the custom of church-going. People had always travelled on a Sunday. Chesterford lay on the route between London and Newmarket; early in the nineteenth century the first day of the Newmarket Spring Meeting was held on Easter Monday, so that more than forty pairs of horses were changed at Chesterford on Easter Day and a regular fair was held there, while the vicar and his congregation were in church celebrating the Resurrection. Bishop Howley took up the matter with the Duke of York, who admitted that he travelled on the Sunday but advanced the extenuating circumstance that he always had a Bible and a Prayer Book with him in his carriage. However, the first day of the meeting was changed from Monday to Tuesday. But the coming of the railways greatly increased the numbers that travelled on a Sunday and encouraged the people of the great cities to take to the sea and countryside on that day, with the consequence that they were absent from their parishes and, therefore, from their parish churches. It seemed fitting retribution to some, therefore, when a train carrying horses and racegoers to Newmarket on a Sunday, fell off an embankment. Some of the public that went by rail, however, went to church at their journey's end, raising problems in seaside parishes with which the vicar of Brighton struggled in an essay on 'Parochial Work in Places of occasional Resort'. He suggested a children's service at nine-thirty a.m. and an afternoon service to lessen the pressure on the evening one.

After the railway came the bicycles, at first the high 'penny-farthing' and then those with wheels of the same size, complete with cyclists on top, some in tight knickerbocker suits and pill-box caps if they belonged to a cycling club. Bicyclists went everywhere, in the last years of the nineteenth century, arriving like a swarm of summer bees in a quiet country village on a Sunday when the villagers were in church or chapel. Randall Davidson devoted part of his charge to the diocese of Winchester in 1899 to the bicyclists and their effect on church-going. He had heard melancholy accounts of the disturbance caused by their arrival in small parishes, thought that the organisers of such outings should take care to avoid the mischief that was caused, and thought, too, that it would be no use simply to denounce as sinful a practice that had come to stay. He regarded bicycling as less mischievous than boating or going by rail since it did not impose extra labour on others, advised the wise parish priest to impress on his own people the duty of worshipping before hopping on to the saddle and suggested that he welcome strangers and provide, if need be, places for bicycles to be stored while their owners were in church.

Yet still in 1900 most incumbents enjoyed good congregations and the sign of the coming storm that would decimate the numbers in the pews was no bigger than a cloud the size of a man's hand when clergy and people advanced into the twentieth century and the old Queen died.

The wealthier of the Queen's subjects liked to enrich their houses with antimacassars, ferns, lace curtains and daguerreotypes in a rich froth that covered their walls and floors and windows. Churches, too, received more elaborate decorations; walls were peppered with stencilled patterns, floors were laid with encaustic tiles, brass made its appearance at the lectern and in the umbrella stands at the end of pews, and the windows were filled with solemn figures in stained glass whose strong colours made the interiors of the churches darker than they had been before, requiring the more frequent use of the oil and gas lamps that had been recently installed. Incumbents, being men of their age, welcomed the introduction of these features, given often in memory of a loved one now departed, and would allow memorials in white marble and in brass recording the achievements of the dead.

Clergy might have a greater responsibility than this, however, if they had charge of the building of a church, for then they might choose their own architect. A few incumbents chose themselves for this task, like the Rev. Whitwell Elwin, who designed the church at Booton in Norfolk where he was the rector, giving it a galaxy of pinnacles and crockets and a quantity of Bath stone; but most went to a reputable architect. Clergy who wanted a riot of decoration might go to Butterfield; those who wanted a bold, blunt church, with a wide nave and narrow aisles, might patronise G. E. Street; evangelicals might go to Ewan Christian and get a dull church, though he was capable of drama as in the roof of Hildenborough church in Kent; those who required good value for their money might employ A. W. Blomfield, forth son of the bishop, who 'excelled in the charitable but unremunerative art of keeping down the cost', or there was Sedding, who used Perpendicular; and Pearson, who used vistas and vaulting; and Bodley, whose ideas were those of the pre-Raphaelites.

For the building of a new church there was usually a committee. Therefore the incumbent, who served on it and might be its chairman, did not have a free hand in its design and construction, even though he might provide a substantial proportion of the cost. H. R. Heywood, son of a rich banker, was appointed to the district chapelry of Swinton in the parish of Eccles in 1864 and arranged that it should become a separate parish. Thereupon he resolved to build a new church at Swinton and engaged Street as his architect, who designed all the details down to the altar-cloth. But there were problems. Land was needed for the extended churchyard, but the land required belonged to a Methodist minister who was reluctant to sell. Heywood went to see him, but found him in bed, and there were protracted negotiations before the land was secured. In a committee debate it was suggested that the new church could be shorter if galleries were allowed, and this led to argument; while a week before its consecration, it was decided that the cross being erected in the reredos should be removed, as being too popish. It was not there for the consecration, and the vicar deprecated its absence in his first sermon in the new church; but he soon had it in its place. The total cost of the church was nearly eighteen thousand pounds, of which the vicar had given more than a quarter. The vicarage box yielded £1. 4s. 8½d. towards the project and the church was opened free of pew rents.[19]

The creation of new churches and the restoration of those that were old, filled with worshippers, organs, choirs, stained glass and bearded vicars, the whole pulsating heavily with life, was a Victorian achievement of considerable magnitude. The church, upon which much time and money, thought and labour, was spent, was the chief setting of an incumbent's work, whether in town or country, and it was here that he addressed his people. The sermon he probably regarded as the climax of his work.

NOTES

1   Addleshaw and Etchells, *The Architectural Setting of Anglican Worship*, pp. 86–7.
2   Henry Phipps Denison, *Seventy-Two Years' Church Recollections*, pp. 7–10.
3   Eric Partridge, *Robert Eyres Landor*, p. 14.
4   J. C. Atkinson, *Forty Years in a Moorland Parish*, p. 44.
5   M. H. Port, *Six Hundred New Churches*, p. 102.
6   Addleshaw and Etchells, *op. cit.*, pp. 93–4.
7   John Sandford, *Parochialia*, p. 40.
8   John Skinner, *Journal of a Somerset Rector*, pp. 200–2.
9   W. C. E. Newbolt, *Speculum Sacerdotum*, p. 41. *Apostles of the Lord*, p. 58. *Priestly Ideals*, p. 95.
10 Flora Thompson, *Lark Rise to Candleford*, p. 210.
11 Michael Reynolds, *Martyr of Ritualism*, pp. 147, 155, 250, 271–3.
12 R. C. D. Jasper, Prayer Book Revision in England, *1800–1900*, pp. 14, 43, 62–3.
13 John C. Miller, *Letters to a Young Clergyman*, p. 186.
14 Ashwell and Wilberforce, *Life of Samuel Wilberforce*, Vol. II,

pp. 289–90.

15 E. S. Talbot, *The Vocation and Dangers of the Church*, p. 29.
16 Hippolyte Taine, *Notes on England*, p. 217.
17 Charles E. Osborne, *The Life of Father Dolling*, pp. 66–70.
18 Hugh McLeod, *Class and Religion in the Late Victorian City*, pp. 104–5.
19 J. Stanley Leatherbarrow, *Victorian Period Piece*, pp. 79–81, 166, 214, 217, 244–5.

CHAPTER 5

The Sermon

BEFORE CLIMBING THE pulpit stairs the clergy of the Church of England had to decide what they were to wear when they gave their sermon, a question of some moment as they well knew. In most places they had put on a surplice for the first part of the service, this being ordered in the canons; but then, after the ante-communion had been said and the time to go into the pulpit had come, they had of necessity to choose whether to continue in the surplice or to remove it and to replace it with a black gown, the surplice being the badge of the high churchmen and the gown being the banner of the evangelicals. Early in the century, and far into it, both customs were to be found. Around 1830 in Guernsey, which was strongly evangelical, not only the sermon but the whole service was conducted by the minister in a gown; but, on the other hand, Dr. Routh, the remarkable president of Magdalen College, Oxford, who acquired the living of Tilehurst near Reading in 1810, preached Townson's sermons, corrected and abridged to a quarter of an hour, in a surplice, being apprehensive of taking cold if he took it off. His precaution proved to be amply justified, for he lived to the age of ninety-nine.

But the advance of the Tractarians and their endeavour to get the clergy into surplices in the pulpit provoked a reaction. In November 1844, Bishop Phillpotts issued a pastoral letter to the clergy of the diocese of Exeter requiring them to take a weekly collection in their churches and to preach in a surplice.

There was uproar and, in the face of fierce opposition, in December, he withdrew the order that the clergy should wear a surplice in the pulpit, leaving the offertory to their discretion. At St. Sidwell's, Exeter, the surplice had already been introduced, not without opposition, by a previous vicar who was later to become a bishop, E. H. Browne, and the next incumbent had continued to use it for the following three years. But the resentment caused by the bishop's directions now boiled over and on going home from church on the evening of January 12th, 1845, the vicar was escorted by a hissing and shouting mob, which reappeared the next Sunday, greatly enlarged and numbering about two thousand, and watched by the entire police force that had been called out on duty. On January 26th the vicar bowed to the storm and preached in a gown. A local paper summed up the incident thus:

> A very pretty public stir
> Is getting up at Exeter
> About the surplice fashion;
> And many angry words and rude
> Have been bestowed upon the feud
> And much unchristian passion.
>
> For me, I neither know nor care
> Whether a parson ought to wear
> A black dress or a white dress,
> Filled with a trouble of my own—
> A wife who lectures in her gown
> And preaches in her nightdress!

Slowly through the 1850s and 60s and 70s the surplice made headway over the gown. Mr. Birch, the rector of Prestwick, Manchester, had been tutor to the Prince of Wales and the more dissenting and radical young ladies of the parish would giggle together before a dinner party while they guessed how many times His Royal Highness would be mentioned during the course of the meal. On Easter Day, 1871, Mr. Birch wore the surplice for the first time in the pulpit and

six years later the choirmen and boys were put into surplices
given by Mrs Birch. Black gowns, however, had not by then
quite disappeared, for when Mrs. Barnett took children from
Whitechapel to a united service at Spitalfields sometime after
1873, she was dismayed to find a terrible parson in a black
gown who, when he lifted his arms, seemed to have black
wings and who descended the first few steps of the pulpit saying 'down, doown, doowwnnn', to describe the fate of the
unconverted child.

The pulpit itself, whether of the 'three-decker' kind or of
the type that stood by itself apart from the reading-desk, was
usually easy to enter and had walls of a suitable height, though
there were exceptions of which visiting preachers needed to
be beware. Hawker at Morwenstow took the panels out of the
pulpit, maintaining that the congregation should be able to
see the preacher's feet, but left the access to it as it was before,
which was by way of a tiny door and up narrow, winding steps.
He argued that it typified the camel going through the eye of a
needle and whispered to preachers as they backed down the
steps after the sermon, 'it is the strait and narrow way and few
there be that find it'. Kilvert went to preach at a harvest festival at Newchurch in Radnorshire and found it difficult to do
so, for though the vicar had assured him that the pulpit would
be almost up to his chin, he found it to be scarcely above his
waist so that, in order to read his sermon, he had to crouch
down in it and lie on one side on the ledge and stick out a leg
behind. Other hazards of preaching were encountered from
time to time, such as the snoring of owls in the belfry, which
sounded like the snoring of people in the gallery. And then
there could be interruptions. A visiting preacher who regularly appeared in the pulpit at St. Paul's, Brighton, on the
feast of the conversion of St. Paul, was stopped one year by a
crazy, middle-aged woman, who started up and cried, 'That is
he! my betrayer, who has deserted me! Come back to me, my
precious, my darling!' The congregation tittering, the woman
was carried out. The preacher required a sedative that night.[1]
At Helmingham, Suffolk, Lord Tollemache attended church
with his servants in their full livery which, in the winter, was of

black with white facings and silver buckles, and in the summer was of white faced with black; he would cut short the sermon by rising to his feet with watch in hand. But the majority of sermons were uneventful, being more productive of sleep than of sensation.

Yet not all slept, by any means. Though there are no statistics on the number of sleepers during sermons in the nineteenth century, the vicar entering the pulpit had in his favour many circumstances which helped to keep awake his congregation. In the first place he was to declare the Word of God; not his own opinions, which might be odd, but the truth as it had been revealed in Scripture. The Anglican clergy had assented to the propositions of the Thirty-Nine Articles of Religion, among which was the assertion that the Holy Scripture contained all things necessary to salvation, so that when they preached, expounding the Bible, they were engaged in a matter of great moment. They were advised, therefore, to read the Bible in its original languages of Hebrew and Greek, and to read it through and thoroughly, for they were assured that it was like the huge pyramids of a distant land—unchanged while all around was changing.[2] At the beginning of the century it indeed seemed to be so, but it was not so at the end, for as the years passed the Bible appeared to be more complex and its truth more difficult for people to discern. Natural science, and especially the revelations of geology concerning the making of the earth over a long time, played havoc with the traditional interpretation of the book of Genesis and its account of the creation of the world in a matter of six days. Bishop Colenso of Natal considered the wanderings of the Israelites in the wilderness, wondered how six men had two-thousand seven hundred and forty-eight sons and how each priest could eat eighty-eight pigeons daily; and so the historical record of the Bible was called in question. And then the moral attitude of the world of the Old Testament seemed, on reflection, to be not wholly worthy. When the book of Exodus decreed that a man striking his slave with his stick so that he died immediately must be punished, but that a man striking his slave who survived a day or two need not be so, it was difficult to see how this could be regarded as an admirable law. The Bible, therefore, required restatement and restatement it duly received, in such works as *Essays and Reviews* where seven clergymen set out to reinterpret the Scripture in the light of the new knowledge that shone upon it; and this, in turn, provoked reaction from those who received it as inerrant in all its details. The reinterpretation was not unsuccessful, but the parochial clergy in their studies, reading books and articles that discussed these things, found that it was becoming more difficult to preach the Bible as utter truth and to commend it to their congregations in that way. Bishop Stubbs of Oxford told his ordination candidates at the end of the century that they need not believe the sun stood still over Gibeon while Joshua took vengeance on the Amorites, and that a good deal of the Bible could only by very indirect ways be regarded as integral to God's revelation.[3] It was advice that would not have been given a hundred years before.

In the absence of more modern media, the Victorian preacher had an attraction that he does not have today. He had few rivals, for though there were political meetings and demonstrations, it was in church and chapel that people were most likely to encounter public speaking. Therefore the sermon had an importance that encouraged a congregation to be attentive for half-an-hour or more. Julius Hare at Hurstmonceux preached for an hour or so to his nodding, rustic villagers, but advisers of the clergy thought that half that time would be enough while some rarely preached for more than twenty minutes. Clergymen enjoyed also a considerable superiority of education over the majority of their parishioners, a fact that was two-edged since, on the one hand, it might give them the respect of their congregations, but, on the other, it might lead them to preach sermons incomprehensible to their people. Julius Hare went straight from Trinity College, Cambridge, to his Sussex parish and, though he tried hard, could not speak naturally and simply to his people, who found his sermons 'mortal long and hard' and misunderstood him. He spoke of the danger of men playing at ninepins with the truth and they thought he was warning young labourers against beer and skittles. But his brother, Augustus, rector of Alton Barnes in Wiltshire, dying in 1834, left behind *Sermons to a Country Congregation* which spoke simply and tersely and in a way the ordinary man could understand: 'Have any of you happened to see the effects of a breeze on a piece of deep water in a sheltered valley? The wind may be sharp enough to ruffle the surface for a while; but the depths of the water are at peace. So it is with the Christian in the world . . .' or 'it is easier to draw the tooth of a child than of a grown-up person, because their teeth have no fangs, as ours have.' Preachers were advised to use words of Anglo-Saxon origin rather than those coming from the Latin, to acquire a command of idiomatic English, to avoid new-fangled words like 'prayerful' and not to speak as though they came from another planet. They should not be high-flown at the beginning, lest people say 'he went up like a rocket and came down like a stick'. They should use metaphor and analogy and anecdote; a startling effect could be produced on a church full of servants on a Sunday afternoon by announcing that God called that person a thief who filched from the tea caddy.

Anecdotes were useful embellishments to a sermon. Bishop Boyd Carpenter of Ripon had noticed in some clergymen's studies a thick, bulky volume, perhaps of a thousand pages or more, with a title such as *Illustrative Anecdotes*, *Pulpit Aids*, or *Fragments of Fancy*. He did not think much of them, observing that they might suit the lame but that they did not strengthen those who could walk. They were, however, popular, and their illustration enlivened many an otherwise rather tedious discourse. One such book, *The Dictionary of Illustrations Adapted to Christian Teaching* was a massive work with a complicated history, for it had begun life as *A Cyclopaedia of Illustrations*, and this had been expanded by the Rev. Elon Foster of New York into *The New Cyclopaedia of Illustrations* which had met with marked success in America among ministers and Sunday school teachers, selling upwards of five thousand copies in less than six months. The work was further revised by the Rev. J. G. Pilkington, the incumbent of St. Mark's, West Hackney, London, who had already compiled *The Spiritual Garland* and had spent twenty years collecting illustrations which were incorporated into a revised and enlarged edition with elaborate textual and topical indexes. By 1882 the book had reached a ninth edition; and the publishers must have been congratulating themselves on their success. Preachers evidently found it full of information, conveniently arranged for their purpose. They could, for example look up 'Persons, Noisy' and read, 'It is with narrow-souled people as with narrow-necked bottles—the less they have in them, the more noise they make in pouring out'. Or they might find the entry, 'Drunkenness, Cure of' and learn of the stout lady, whose husband went home so drunk that he had to go immediately to bed. She sewed him up in a blanket; then took a cowhide and with all her strength commenced beating the dust out of the blanket and the rum out of her husband. Yells and screams came from the blanket, but had no effect till the husband was thoroughly sobered. The effect was good, for that was the end of his drunkenness. Or, preaching on marriage, they might find the subject treated in 'Marriage, Danger of' and be reminded of the wise frogs in Aesop who had a great mind for some water, yet would not leap into the well because they could not get out again.

The use of anecdotes and illustrations had to be carefully handled, else they might themselves be remembered—or mis-remembered—while the point that they were supposed to make was forgotten. A vicar imagined a conversation in a London boudoir between three young ladies just back from church and their mother, who had been prevented from going because of the tooth-ache. The young ladies raved about the preacher and came to the subject of the illustrations to his sermon:

Alice:	There were some striking anecdotes.
Kate:	Yes, that one about the bear, for instance. A Laplander was once pursuing a bear—
Eva:	Now, Kate! the bear was pursuing *him*!

Kate: Well, it was one way or the other; and the Lap-
          lander had a Bible in his breast-pocket which his
          mother had given him.
Eva: No, his grandmother.
Alice: It was not a Laplander at all. You are confusing it
          with another anecdote. It was a young English
          sailor.
Kate: Well, Laplander, or English sailor, or whatever
          he was, he was just close to the bear, when—
Eva: You are missing out the best part of the story.
          Before he started, his grandmother said to him—
Kate: Ah, yes; but, if you remember, he had first said to
          his grandmother—
Eva: You are quite wrong.
Kate: Do let me go on. At all events, he and his
          grandmother had been talking together—
Alice: You forget, Kate, that the grandmother was deaf
          and dumb. That was the touching part of the
          story. So she pointed to the Bible—
Kate: Nonsense, Alice, I am sure the grandmother—
Mother: I am afraid, dears, you will not make much of that
          anecdote.[4]

If the use of anecdotes had to be carefully considered, so
did the technique of preaching, and this was a major concern
of Charles Simeon, the notable evangelical vicar of Holy Trinity, Cambridge, who gave classes in sermon composition to
undergraduates in his rooms at King's College. He warned
them to beware of laying emphasis on every word or with
great frequency, suggesting that it was better to group a sen-
tence together by rapid speech and to mark the emphasis by
pausing between the more emphatic parts. It was good, when
speaking, to address some inanimate object, a chair or inkstand, door or pillar. 'I preach usually to the small door in the
west gallery of Trinity Church: it is a good central spot for me
to direct my countenance to; it is a fair average of the more
distant parts of the congregation. When I perceive that the
door distinctly hears me, then I know that all the congregation

may'[5] It was better to speak from the tongue, lips and teeth, than from the chest and throat; and better to use the natural voice. R. W. Evans, vicar of Heversham, Westmorland, advised against shouting; it reminded a congregation more of a priest of Baal than of a minister of Christ. Some preachers got up steam as deliberately and mechanically as a locomotive so that you could almost hear the piling on of the coke and the manipulation of the handles. Their words came whirling, tumbling, seething and hissing out; they might faint away afterwards in the vestry and need to be revived by having their temples covered with brown paper, dipped in brandy.

Other dangers to be avoided were the grotesque use of texts and the employment of pet phrases. The preacher who attacked the extravagant head-dresses of his day with the text of Scripture, 'Topnot, come down', had certainly discovered a striking application of some words from the Bible, but it was absurd to wrench them from the Lord's description of the future and the warning, 'Let them that are on the housetop not come down'. A pet phrase, too, could be dangerous, for once it had been used it might allow the congregation to be lulled into a sense of security and go to sleep. Sermons using this technique were like a rabbit-hunt, in which there is a scratching and a scrambling and a flinging up of the dirt, and then suddenly the coming out of the terrier with the wretched dead rabbit.[6]

Because the sermon was so important, much preparation of it was required. John Gott, Dean of Worcester, suggested that its major part should be written on the knees; another told the clergy that they should not regret spending five or six hours on a composition listened to by scarcely a score of rustics. After a little experience, four or five hours might be sufficient, perhaps, for a sermon lasting short of half-an-hour. On Good Friday, 1870, Kilvert breakfasted at eight and spent till nine-thirty writing his Easter sermon; the next day he rose soon after five and continued with it for another two hours. Christopher Wordsworth recalled how his father would stroll about the fields on a Saturday morning and speak his sermon for the following day to the fields and hedges. Not all preachers were as conscientious as these, however, and thought they were advised not to use other people's sermons, nevertheless some did, continuing a practice firmly established in the previous century. Then an enterprising clergyman, John Trusler, circulated every parish in England and Ireland with a proposal to print in script type, in imitation of handwriting, one hundred and fifty sermons at the price of a shilling each, and met with considerable success.

But the consequences of using other people's sermons were not always foreseen. A curate preached a sermon one Sunday morning while a brother curate was preaching at a chapel-of-ease, only in the evening to hear his brother curate preach the sermon he had delivered that morning to the same congregation. Arthur Roberts, rector of Woodrising in Norfolk for fifty-five years, published seventeen volumes of village sermons which were widely used; when there was an eclipse of the sun he happened to be on holiday and heard his sermon for the occasion preached in two churches. Baring-Gould was dogged at one time by an evidently popular sermon on 'Felix trembling'. Visiting his uncle, he beseeched him not to preach on Felix, who had trembled in Hurst Chapel a few Sundays back, and the Sunday after in a church at Brighton till his teeth chattered, and then at Teignmouth where he appeared again like a jack-in-the-box. A year later uncle and nephew were in the same church in Devon when the uncle, who was intending to preach the Felix sermon, remembered the previous conversation and, finding that he had Blind Bartimeus in his other pocket, pulled him out and shot him off.

It was estimated in the 1880s that fifty thousand sermons a week were preached in England and Wales by the clergy of the National Church and people asked anxiously what this considerable volume of oratory achieved. The answer was not clear but it was evident that in such a number of sermons there would be great variety. There were sermons which were all bones, the structure on which they had been composed being left rigorously clear; and there were sermons that were amoeba-like in their fluidity, having apparently no form at all. There were dull sermons, apathetic sermons, sermons in which neither preacher nor congregation took much interest; and some of the clergy, fearful of the excitements offered by preachers in the dissenting chapels, cultivated a style that was deliberately low-key, against which Sydney Smith protested:

> Why call in the aid of paralysis of piety? Is sin to be taken from men, as Eve was from Adam, by casting them into a deep slumber? Or from what possible perversion of common sense are we all to look like field-preachers in Zembla, holy lumps of ice, numbed into quiescence and stagnation and mumbling? Is it theatrical to use action, and is it methodistical to use action? But we have cherished contempt for sectaries, and persevered in dignified tameness so long, that while we are freezing common sense for large salaries in stately churches, amidst whole acres and furlongs of empty pews, the crowd are feasting on ungrammatical fervour and illiterate animation in the crumbling hovels of Methodists.[7]

Besides the alteration in the attitude to the Bible, which was found in the nineteenth century, there was a difference in the tone of the sermons that were delivered then. In the eighteenth century, Anglican preachers spoke of the excellence of the Christian religion, the reasonableness of its precepts and the necessity of right conduct; but their successors, reacting against this cool, rational faith, turned in other directions. Evangelicals would preach on the merits of the blood of Christ, on justification by faith, on the need for personal conversion; and Tractarians would preach on the saints and the sacraments and the Church as the body of Christ. G. R. Prynne, who was a notable Tractarian in the West of England and incumbent for many years of St. Peter's, Plymouth, where he suffered from much opposition in his early days and was once threatened by a riotous crowd demanding that he should be hung from a lamp-post, preached the same sermon on the fiftieth anniversary of his appointment to the parish as the first that he had given there as vicar, thereby demonstrating the consistency of his teaching. But neither evangelicals nor

Tractarians remained exclusively with their particular themes, unless they were very narrow-minded, and they and many others were alike affected by the reaction from class-icism towards a more warmly-felt form of faith.

For the Victorians were not afraid to appeal to the emo-tions, rejecting the preaching of 'cold Christs and tangled Trinities'. It was not the sinlessness of the Redeemer, nor His unconquerable fidelity to duty, nor His superhuman noble-ness that made people wish to follow Him, but rather it was the knowledge that He wept at the grave of friendship, that He shrank from the sharpness of death and knew the feeling of human doubt which swept across His soul like a desolation that made Him human and, therefore, the example for men to follow. Christ had all the natural appetites of the body; relax-ation and friendship were dear to Him, and so were sunlight and life. The tear would start from His eyes at the sight of human sorrow. St. Paul, too, was human. We see in him a frail and struggling apostle, a man who could say, 'Brethren, I count not myself to have apprehended'.

These are the words of one of the great nineteenth-century preachers of the Church of England, F. W. Robertson. He belonged to no party in the Church, had no great patron and received no preferment, but ministered at the small prop-rietary Trinity Chapel at Brighton until his early death aged thirty-seven, in 1853, which was hastened by his support of the revolutionary ideas of 1848 and the opposition that that support aroused. When Adelaide, the Queen Dowager, died in 1849, desiring to give as little trouble as possible and requesting that her body be neither dissected nor embalmed, Robertson preached a sermon for this special occasion on 'The Israelites Grave in a Foreign Land'. He spoke of Joseph, but began with words designed to catch the attention of his congregation: 'There is a moment when a man's life is relived on earth. It is in that hour in which the coffin lid is shut down, just before the funeral, when earth has seen the last of him for ever. Then the whole life is, as it were, lived over again in the conversation which turns upon the memory of the departed.' The sermon goes on to speak of Joseph's life, of his goodness, and of how he, a foreigner, saved Egypt from the scourge of famine. It tells of Joseph's death and how every man in Egypt felt then that he had lost a friend, drawing a comparison with the departed Queen who, like Joseph, was a foreigner and, like Joseph, good. Yet he does not flatter, which is always a temptation on such occasions, and points beyond the Queen to the source of such merits as she possessed; and so he leaves his congregation: 'All that she had she received. If we honour her, it is to adore Him who made her what she was. Of His fulness she had received, and grace for grace.'[8]

The other great preacher who as an incumbent regularly occupied the pulpit in the nineteenth century was J. H. Newman in his Anglican days, for as vicar of the Church of St. Mary-the-Virgin at Oxford, the University church, he preached regularly to his parishioners, chiefly dons and undergraduates but with a sprinkling of business and professional people as well. He spoke at four o'clock on a Sunday afternoon, at a time when most of the colleges had dinner, and, since most men preferred a warm dinner without Newman's sermon to a cold one with it, the large church was little more than half filled. The service was very simple. The sermon was read and, in the winter, delivered with the gaslight by the pulpit lowered, so that the preacher might not be dazzled; it was given without vehemence or declamation or intellectual pyrotechnics, and a Scottish town congregation, it was suggested, would have thought the preacher a 'silly body'. The language used was unadorned, yet wonderfully modulated; the voice calm and musical. But the profound impression that he made was due in large measure not to these things but to his pyschological insight and evident holiness. He understood, it seemed, the temptations of tradesmen, their predisposition to avarice and the making of a fortune, though he was not himself in their situation nor tempted that way. His holiness, too, was evident. Matthew Arnold in later years seemed to hear him saying still, 'After the fever of life, after weariness and sickness, fightings and despondings, languor and fretfulness, struggling and succeeding; after all the changes and chances of this troubled unhealthy state at length comes death, at length the white throne of God, at length the beatific vision.'

The sermons at Oxford were published in eight volumes under the title *Parochial and Plain Sermons*. They are marked by a reticence of feeling, though the feeling is there, a preference for moral rather than doctrinal subjects, and the choice of a text that could be considered from many different angles. To give but one example, here is Newman on holiness:

Which of our tastes and likings can we change at our will in a moment? Not the most superficial. Can we then at a word change the whole frame and character of our minds? Is not holiness the result of many patient, repeated efforts after obedience, gradually working on us, and first modifying and then changing our hearts? We dare not, of course, set bounds to God's mercy and power in cases of repentance late in life, even where He has revealed to us the general rule of His moral governance; yet, surely it is our duty ever to keep steadily before us, and act upon, those general truths which His holy Word has declared. His holy Word in various ways warns us, that, as no one will find happiness in heaven, who is not holy, so no one can learn to be so, in a short time, and when he will.[9]

Few, very few, could preach like Robertson or Newman, and in the majority of parishes sermons were on a much lower level. Preachers might mount their hobby horses, giving them frequent Sunday airings, and at times it seemed that a policeman had got into the pulpit. Bishop Mant in Ireland suggested that acts of outrage in the nieghbourhood and lawless assaults upon the property or life of others, especially when the culprits were caught and conviction followed, gave opportunity to remind the faithful of the terrors of the divine law, as well as of the human, which might fall upon the transgressors. The clergy might be fervent upholders of the *status quo*, like the old rector in *Lark Rise to Candleford*, who preached frequently on the supreme rightness of the social order as it then existed. God, in His infinite wisdom, had appointed a place for all and it was their duty to stay in their niches. Gentlemen had to pay taxes, sit on the Bench, oversee their estates and entertain. Could labourers do that? No, of course not. Neither could a gentleman cut a straight furrow or mow or thatch or rick as they could. So the workers should be thankful and rejoice in their strength and the bounty of the farmer who found them work and paid them. When Gladstone was returned as Prime Minister of a Liberal government at the age of eighty-two, at the general election of 1886, the rector flushed with anger in the pulpit, his frost-blue eyes flashing like swords, and roared, 'There are some among you who have lately forgotten that duty, and we know the cause, the *bloody* cause.' But few had listened. 'I must've been nodding,' one said. The rector's successor was different, used local matter and the papers to illustrate his theme, did not speak of hell and described the earth as not a bad place after all, if people would share their burdens and pull together.

Vice was a popular subject with congregations, for at least everyone knew what that was about. Canon Newbolt wanted a sermon at least once a year on each of the vices, lust, drunkenness, untruthfulness, dishonesty and other common sins, but thought that when impurity was to be the theme, refined ladies and children should be warned beforehand so that they might absent themselves. He was not sure that a Sanitation Sunday, with the emphasis on drains, was edifying, for it might lead to a lowering of the Christian pulpit. Some wanted sermons on topics of the day. 'We are living in this reckless, rushing, helter-skelter nineteenth century, and our parsons should select their subjects accordingly,' was one view put forward, while others wanted sermons on science, or sermons in defence of Christianity. Yet others wanted the Bible simply explained to them. It would not be monotonous for the Bible was like a magnificent kaleidoscope and the preacher's job was to shake it gently so that it produced endless combinations of exquisite form and beauty.[10] The festivals of the Church provided subjects for sermons also, and though Christmas and Easter might not be difficult to deal with, Trinity Sunday might give a headache to the preacher who must preach on that occasion. When E. H. Browne preached at Fen Ditton one Trinity Sunday, an old woman stopped him after to thank him for his beautiful sermon, 'for', she said, quite earnestly, 'I never did see so clear before how there were three Gods.'

From the pulpits of the nineteenth century, then, there thundered the sound of many voices delivering many sermons. There were long ones lasting an hour or more, and short ones of ten minutes. There were good ones and bad ones, and those that were comprehensible and those that were not. They might be given extempore, though they had been carefully prepared, or they might be given extempore because no time or thought had been given to them. They might be written out, or they might be the words of another preacher, perhaps even one long dead. They might be full of splendid prose or composed in the rough style of the fox-hunting parson. A great volume of oratory poured down Sunday by Sunday on the faithful, until the day came when they were carried in their coffins for the last time to the church and heard nothing of the service, though in their lifetime they had heard so much.

NOTES

1   S. Baring-Gould, *Early Reminiscences 1834–1864*, p. 284.
2   J. R. Woodford, *The Great Commission*, p. 39.
3   William Stubbs, *Ordination Addresses*, pp. 41–6.
4   Henry Twells, *Collequies on Preaching*, pp. 77–8.
5   Charles Smyth, *The Art of Preaching*, ch. 5.
6   W. Boyd Carpenter, *Lectures on Preaching*, pp. 99, 106–7.
7   J. H. Overton, *The English Church in the Nineteenth Century*, p. 139.
8   F. W. Robertson, *Sermons Preached at Brighton First Series*, pp. 304–22.
9   J. H. Newman, *Parochial and Plain Sermons*, Vol. 1, p. 12.
10 Henry Twells, *op. cit.*, pp. 45–56.

CHAPTER 6

The Dead

WHEN ARCHBISHOP TAIT began his second visitation of the diocese of Canterbury he spoke to the foundation members of its cathedral, which included the choristers and the young scholars of the King's School there, and prayed, 'God grant that, as the end cannot be very far off, even for the youngest of us, as it is very near for the oldest, we may all be getting ready for the great Assize.' Death was very evident in the nineteenth century, and much discussed, even with children. Mrs. Alexander, who gave to the world the children's hymns, 'There is a green hill far away' and 'All things bright and beautiful', wrote many others, among which there was one that told the young about the dead. She included it in *Hymns for Little Children*, published in 1848, from whence it passed into the standard edition of *Hymns Ancient and Modern* in 1875. It contained the words:

> Within the churchyard, side by side,
>   Are many long, low graves;
> And some have stones set over them,
>   On some the green grass waves.
>
> Full many a little Christian child,
>   Woman and man, lies there;
> And we pass near them every time
>   When we go in to prayer.

> They do not hear when the great bell
>   Is ringing overhead;
> They cannot rise and come to Church
>   With us, for they are dead.

She very properly went on to speak of the hope of resurrection, yet it was not one of her happier attempts at hymn writing even though it reflected the Victorian acknowledgment of death with which children also were expected to be familiar.

Kingsley often spoke of death. 'Oh! how blessed it will be when it is all over, to lie down in that dear churchyard,' he would say, when a letter had been written, or a chapter of a book had been finished, or a page of a sermon had been completed, and this at the age of thirty-one. Kilvert, appointed vicar of Bredwardine, on the Wye in Herefordshire, in 1877, walked in the churchyard within three months of his arrival to choose a place for his grave, not knowing that, though he was only thirty-seven, he would die of peritonitis nineteen months later.

Death was an important element in Victorian life. Vicars and rectors, who administered the last rites, who commended to God the departed and who buried the dead and decided where in the church or churchyard they should lie, were naturally more preoccupied with death than many others. In the first half of the century, in the towns, the problems of burial grew to huge proportions as the population rapidly increased and the number of the dying multiplied; while the churches and the churchyards, situated in confined spaces, could not grow. A parish or two like St. Pancras bought extra land, but few could do this, so that when the dead poured in it was difficult to find for them accommodation. Gravediggers, it was suspected, dug up coffins and sold their lead and wood, thus making more room in the crammed churchyards; a gravedigger at St. Anne's, Soho, played skittles with the skulls; the dead seemed everywhere.[1] At St. Mary-le-Bow, Wren had closed the Norman crypt when he rebuilt the church, using it as the foundation of his new building, not wanting it to be a burial place; but a burial place it was in the eighteenth and nineteenth centuries. At last the government was forced to act and, by the Public Health Act of 1848 and the Cemetery Acts of 1852 and 1853, made it possible to create new public cemeteries on the edges of the towns and to close old ones, so that the dead now went by train to their resting places. Father Mackonochie, who had done such valiant work at St. Alban's, Holborn, was not buried there but in Woking Cemetery, where his parish had a plot that was reserved for its parishioners.

An epidemic of a disease like cholera raised problems also. Since no one knew the cause of it, no one wanted to approach its victims nor to have them buried near at hand; and the sudden increase in the number of the dead resulting from its visitation placed a strain on the resources of the town or village to which it came. In 1832 the cholera reached Camerton, where a boy and his grandmother died of the disease. The rector thereupon had a deep grave dug, out of line with the others but within the churchyard, and told the clerk to purchase from the public house a bottle of spirits which was to be given to those who conveyed the bodies to the grave. He determined to take the funerals himself. In the same year the cholera was at Exeter, where a remote spot in the parish of St. David's was hurriedly licensed as a burial ground, and there a hut was built for the clergy to shelter in between the funerals, which were so frequent that a rota was arranged in order that one of them was always there on duty. The night shift, when few people were about, proved to be the busiest.[2]

In the country there was usually space enough in the churchyard for the burial of the dead, and if the churchyard was full, then it was easy enough to take in more land and to extend it. At Eversley the parish wanted the rick-yard of the glebe for an extension, to which Kingsley agreed, reminding himself that he was not a king, that the parishioners were a corporation of free men who had a right to their own opinion, and that it was a most blessed thing that it was so. In this new part he decided to be buried and spent many hours there with

a faithful farmer planting it with evergreens. At Langley Burrell there was a lack of space and the digging of one grave
there brought the winter's water pouring in from its
neighbour, releasing a deadly stench. The wall between the
graves was probably too thin, but the churchyard had little
room to spare. Bishops sometimes turned their attention to
the churchyard, like Bishop Otter who advised his clergy of
the diocese of Chichester to keep a large map of their
churchyard in the vestry. More romantically, it was suggested
by one clergyman that they should be planted with evergreens
and a few low shrubs—cedar of Lebanon, cypress, the red and
white cedar, the common and Irish yew, the holly, the laurus-
tinus, the juniper, the Fulham and the Luccombe oaks, the
broom, the oriental *arbor vitae.* The decking of the graves
with flowers, a pleasant occupation for a Saturday or Sunday
afternoon, was not common before the third quarter of the
century.

The important people of the parish were buried in the
church or in vaults built in the churchyard, for just as they had
received respect in life, so in death they expected to receive
more honoured resting places. But by the nineteenth century
the space beneath the church was often full of the bones of
previous parishioners, making it difficult to find room for new
interments. John Lewis Bythesea was rector of Bagendon in
Gloucestershie from 1800 to 1845 and employed a curate
who was called upon from time to time to undertake strange
duties. When the rector's brother died one day visiting the
parish, the curate was asked to take a spade and to dig in the
chancel of the church until he found a space beneath the floor
for the burial of the brother. The curate returned, reporting
that the chancel floor was full of departed rectors, to which
Bythesea replied, 'Tut, tut, Henry; scrabble them all on one
side; and while you are doing it, make room for me, too.'[3] At
Ketteringham, Sir John Boileau, seeing that his wife was ill,
thought of her burial place and, having been given the key of
the chancel vault of the church when he had purchased the
advowson of the living with the estate, decided to investigate
it further. Early one morning, taking his carpenter, he

unlocked the vault and the carpenter went down the steps to find the vault was full and that it could not be enlarged. Sir John resolved to move its occupants into the churchyard, consulted the bishop who advised that the plan might be illicit but could be carried out if done surreptitiously, and paid a visit to the vicar, leaving him a sovereign for making a new grave in the churchyard for the remains. The bodies thereupon were moved, releasing a deadly stench which on the Sunday following had to be fought with chloride of lime before the congregation assembled. But some of the bodies so disturbed were those of the recently departed; and their living relations, having heard of the idignity suffered by their predecessors, did not let the matter rest when they came to hear of it. Sir John was forced, therefore, to move the remains back into the chancel and to construct a mausoleum in the churchyard for his family. The vicar was paid twenty-five pounds for its construction but since he had not told Sir John that some of the burials in the chancel vault were of recent date, which was a fact that he knew well, relations between the squire and vicar were strained.[4]

Vicars and rectors, or their deputies, conducted the services in the church and churchyards, the burial service among them. The parishioner had the right to be buried within the churchyard of his parish church, unless he had committed suicide, or was excommunicate or unbaptised; but none had the right to have a minister officiate who was not Anglican. In the country, therefore, where the churchyard was usually the only burial place, dissenters must be buried there, not by their own minister but by the vicar of the church. How much resentment was caused by this is difficult to say, but there was sufficient for the matter to be raised in Parliament. The Anglican clergy were willing to allow a burial in silence in the churchyard for a nonconformist, were willing to take a service with words of Scripture to which no nonconformist could object, were willing to allow hymns but were not willing to allow nonconformist ministers to officiate. The battle raged fiercely until 1880 when the Burial Law Amendment Act ordered that relatives might give notice to the incumbent that the deceased would be buried without the Prayer Book service and allowed that the service at the grave might be such as the relatives saw fit, provided it was orderly and Christian. No one could give an address that brought into contempt the Christian religion or members or ministers of any other denomination. Christopher Wordsworth called it an 'Act for the martyrdom of the National Church under the narcotic influences of chloroform', but his language was extravagant. No disaster ensued and the Act brought peace. Bishop Mackarness, in the year following its passing, advised the clergy of the diocese of Oxford to work the Act as smoothly as possible, allowing the bell to be tolled where it would have been tolled before and allowing the use of the bier without regard to the nature of the religious service to be said at the grave.

Burials were followed by memorials in churches and tombstones in churchyards, for it was pleasant to commemorate the dead and to record their names and achievements for posterity: but incumbents had control over their erection and could at least attempt to veto inscriptions that they thought not to be suitable. At Owston Ferry in Lincolnshire in 1874 the youngest daughter of a Wesleyan minister died at the age of seven and the father wished to place an inscription on the tombstone which would inform all those who saw it that she was the daughter of the 'Reverend H. Keet, Wesleyan minister'. The vicar did not think that in a churchyard a Wesleyan minister might be described as 'Reverend', and he was supported by his bishop, Christopher Wordsworth, who the previous year had angered the Wesleyans by addressing a pastoral letter to them in which he expatiated on the perils of schism and the blessings of unity. The lower courts upheld the vicar and the bishop, but the Judicial Committee of the Privy Council reversed their decisions and on the tombstone the word 'Reverend' went. In another case the Court of Arches ruled that the incumbent had no power to exclude an inscription because it read, 'Pray for the soul of J. Woolfrey. It is a holy and wholesome thought to pray for the dead', since no canon or authority of the Church had expressly prohibited the practice of praying for the dead.

Funerals might be large and expensive, like that of Peter Featherstone described in *Middlemarch*, which was enriched with three mourning-coaches, pall-bearers on horseback with the richest scarves and hatbands, and under bearers also with good, well-priced trappings of woe, all in black. Or they might be simple, with the coffin brought to church, either on a bed of straw laid in a farm waggon freshly painted or newly scrubbed, or on a wheeled hand-bier. The priest met the funeral procession at the churchyard gate and led it, as the Prayer Book said, either into the church or towards the grave, reading sentences of Scripture as he went. The Overseer of Falmouth complained in 1832 that the fee to the clergyman for a pauper's funeral was one shilling and sixpence but that an extra five shillings had to be paid if the body was taken into church. The service could have its difficulties. An incumbent might face the problem of a man who died in a fit of intoxication, fighting in a public house. Was it right to read the service over him, who was a notorious evil-liver, and yet who had an undoubted right to be buried in the churchyard since he had been baptised and had not been excommunicated and had not died by his own hand? A neighbouring clergyman, it was suggested, might be asked to take the service in this case, though some vicars might prefer to officiate themselves and preach on the shortcomings of the departed. Kilvert heard a story of how Parson Williams of Llanbedr preached such a sermon at the funeral of a farmer with whom he had quarrelled and used the text, 'Hell from beneath is moved for thee to meet thee at thy coming'.

The Church's service for the burial of the dead was not for the unbaptised, since they were not members of the Church; yet many in the great cities had never been brought as infants to baptism and had never managed to receive that sacrament in their later years, though they regarded themselves as Christian and members of the Church of England. It was a matter of distress, then, to relatives of the departed when they found that the unbaptised deceased could not be sent upon their way with the blessing of the Church, and it might distress kind-hearted clergymen, too, who had to refuse to use the service.

One remedy suggested was for the parish priest to be ready at all times and without scruple to administer private baptism. Another was to instruct intelligent laymen in the towns, such as doctors, churchwardens, lay-readers, schoolmasters, how to baptise. Convocation ruled that it was permissible, after the unbaptised had been laid in the earth, for prayers and Scripture readings to be used round the grave, though not the burial and the communion services. On the principle that ignorance is bliss, some clergy did not ask whether the deceased had been baptised.

Seaside parishes had a grisly duty laid upon them to bury bodies washed up on their shores, which was unpleasant at the best of times, but especially so if they had been a long time in the sea or cut to pieces on the rocks. Hawker naturally enough hated taking funerals at Morwenstow.

NOTES

1   Owen Chadwick, *The Victorian Church*, Part 1, pp. 326–7.
2   Norman Longmate, *King Cholera*, p. 131.
3   William Addison, *The English Country Parson*, p. 175.
4   Owen Chadwick, *Victorian Miniature*, ch. 8.

CHAPTER 7

Visiting

'THE COUNTRY PARSON upon the afternoons in the week-days takes occasion sometimes to visit in person, now one quarter of his parish, now another. For there he shall find his flock most naturally as they are, wallowing in the midst of their affairs.' George Herbert's words show that the visiting parson, tramping down the streets or lanes of his parish or moving about on horseback, ubiquitous and frequent in his appearances, knocking on the doors of parishioners rich and poor, sick and well, religious and irreligious, was an ideal that went back a long way in the history of the Church.

It was not, however, an ideal that went unchallenged, nor an ideal that was always carried into practice in the nineteenth century, though it was accepted more widely and carried out more fully than in the century before.

When vicars and rectors were non-resident or absent for many months at a time from their parishes, enjoying a Mediterranean tour or the fashionable watering-places of England, it was clear that they could not visit their parishioners. A curate, put in charge of such a parish, might ride over from a neighbouring town to take Sunday duty, but he was a bird of passage, available one day in the week and not otherwise, able to deal with matters brought to his attention but, in the nature of the case, not knowing the people well since he did not see them working in the week. But the increasing residence of the parochial clergy in their parishes after 1800 brought them inevitably into closer contact with their people; and though they might not visit diligently or systematically even when they lived in their parishes, yet the mere fact of their propinquity meant that they saw more of them, for much can be learned from a well-placed vicarage window.

Some laypeople were uneasy over persistent and thorough visiting by the clergy, fearing that it led to a society dominated by priests, in which people came to feel 'big brother is watching you'. Randall Davidson, then Dean of Windsor, remembered how Queen Victoria had a quite extraordinary fear of clericalism and discouraged any really pastoral relationship with members of her household. She advised him not to visit too much, even her old coachman, though he liked the dean to come when he was ill.[1] Clergy in visiting might conduct an inquiry which came near to being an inquisition. Have they Bibles and Prayer Books?—the clergy were advised to ask. 'Are they confirmed? How far do they study the Bible privately? And why are they habitually late for church?' An arrogant clergyman could make those he visited distinctly uncomfortable, even though he did not have the power to burn them at the stake. The Brontës at Haworth 'kept themselves close' and Patrick Brontë did no regular visiting, though he visited the sick and those who sent for him; and this approach seems to have been appreciated, for an inhabitant of a district near Haworth described his clergyman as 'a rare good one. He minds his own business, and ne'er troubles himself with ours.'

Others maintained that too frequent visits meant that they became commonplace and unwelcome. The arrival of the vicar on the doorstep, some said, should bring with it a sense of occasion, like the arrival of royalty in the neighbourhood. Going into cottages too often meant that the vicar lost that respect and consideration for his visits, which were necessary if they were to be given their proper influence. Nor was it necessary to be continually in and out of houses, because a parish might be served as well without a constant parochial perambulation. Dean Merivale remarked on Alford's ministry at Wymeswold:

the habits of the people did not demand, nor perhaps did the usage of the clerical school in which he had been trained suggest, the constant house-to-house visitation which might be looked for in rural parishes for these days; but he carried on three full services single-handed every Sunday, he built and superintended his schools, he almost rebuilt his church, and his earnestness and evident self-sacrifice won him the unbounded love of his parishioners.[2]

Given the immense gulf that then existed between a gentleman and the labouring classes it is hardly surprising that some of the clergy found it difficult to grasp the working of the minds of those who earned a meagre pittance with their hands, so that a vicar coming to a cottage might seem to its inhabitants like a man from the moon. A parishioner at Hurstmonceux, Archdeacon Hare's parish, reported, 'the Archdeacon he do come to us, and he do sit by the bed and hold our hands, but he do zay nowt'. The future Dean Church went to the parish of Whatley in Somerset, a most unsuitable appointment, at the age of thirty-eight, with no parochial experience, frail, undersized, studious, his head full of Dante and Anselm. The unathletic pastor organised regular paper chases for the village boys and long country walks in summer for the older children who searched for wild flowers, but after four years of visiting he admitted frankly that he could not understand his people. 'To me,' he wrote in 1857, 'they seem to live in impenetrable shells of their own; now and then you seem to pinch them or to please them, but I can never find out the rule that either goes by. I think sometimes whether one ought not to give up reading, and all communication with the world one has been accustomed to, in order to try and get accustomed to theirs—but this does not seem a promising plan either. I hope that something tells, though one does not see the way how.'[3] When Flora Thompson's rector went visiting in her hamlet the cottagers closed up like clams. He would go from cottage to cottage, working his way round from door to door, calling upon everybody. A tap with his

gold-headed cane brought a scuffling within as unseemly
objects were hustled out of sight. The rector sat and the hos-
tess sat, and they discussed the weather, the health of the family, the absent children, the pig, the allotment, but not religion. It was regarded in the parish as one of his great virtues
that he did not discuss religion. But the gulf was wide between
him and his people and though he meant well, neither he nor
they could bridge it. The kindly enquiries made and answered, he would rise to go and be shown out with alacrity.

The gulf between the classes meant that some of the clergy
were tempted unthinkingly to ride roughshod over their
parishioners. Therefore they had to be reminded that their
people had feelings and were entitled to consideration; cottagers were not like the cattle of the fields. Canon Newbolt in
describing the gentle life of the priest found it necessary to
mention that when the priest went round his parish visiting he
should have the courtesy to knock on the door and wait to be
invited in. Others advised him to take off his hat when entering a peasant's hut and not to take a chair unless it had first
been offered. It was regarded as a virtue of John Allen that
when he went visiting in his parish of Prees near Shrewsbury
he would withdraw if a meal happened to be in progress: a
parishioner recalled, 'If ever he came when we were at meals,
he would never come in, he would say, "O you are at your tea
or dinner—I won't come in, thank you—are you all well," and
if by chance we were out, we knew when he had been, by a
Cross he always made in the sand.(*sic*)".'⁴

Domestic servants comprised one class of the poor which it
was especially difficult to reach, since it was necessary to
approach them through their employers, and their employers
might not be agreeable to the clergy coming into the back
quarters of their homes. Bishops, before leaving the country
seats of the landed gentry with whom they often stayed, might
ask if they could address the servants and could hardly be
refused; but the parochial clergy had not such authority. Burgon in his parish at Oxford found that he could reach some
servants by going round in the morning while the maids were
washing the doorsteps, saying 'Good morning' and adding a

few words about the weather, though not enough to detain them from their duties. Then, pressing a tract into their hands, he would remark that he would be coming that way again sometime and perhaps then they would have a little talk about it.

Not all agreed that the lower classes were the most difficult to visit, for some thought that the approach to the middle class presented more problems. Labourers and their families recognised the disparity of rank between the clergy and themselves, but this disparity was not so great between the clergy and the middle class, who were only a little lower in the social scale than most vicars and rectors and might resent the fact. 'The middle class,' Manning thought, 'is not penetrated by the pastoral ministry—as the upper class by kindred and association, and the lower by direct instruction and oversight.' The remedy was a greater pastoral humility and simplicity for incumbents visiting farmers in the country and business men in the towns. Few thought it wise or right to put the ministry of the Church into the hands of those who were less than gentlemen in order to meet this challenge and the lowering of the social status of the clergy was eventually largely brought about by their deteriorating economic situation.

With those of the highest grade most incumbents mixed on equal terms so visiting was easy. A vicar might be the brother of the squire and a rector the nephew of the largest local landowner, and where there was no blood relationship there was an affinity brought about by education, custom and wealth. Observing the English scene, Taine saw that priest and layman were on a single footing, or separated at most by a single step, and wrongly concluded that this was the principle achievement of the Reformation. It seemed to him that by education, marriage, mores and function, the clergy were laymen, a little graver in bearing than the rest, and outside church distinguished only by the wearing of the eternal white tie. The contrast with France was very striking. When Samuel Wilberforce stayed with Guizot in 1870 his host remarked that he could not have stayed for a week in a country house in England without meeting the rector of the parish, but that in

France he could not ask any *cure* in the district to his table.

The total, systematic visiting of all the healthy parishioners in a parish by its incumbent was rendered impossible when the parish was very large, and unnecessary when it was very small. It was obvious at Leeds that Hook could not visit all his parishioners so he let it be known that he was ready to receive the poor at ten a.m. In other large parishes, where a staff of curates could be afforded, the work of visiting would be delegated to them and this then could be undertaken on a comprehensive scale. Archbishop Garbett recalled how he went to Portsea as a curate in 1899 and that he and his fellow curates were taught to visit for four hours on five days of the week; but Portsea was exceptional in the size of its staff and most large parishes did not have curates available who could knock on every door. Lay district visitors were therefore sometimes used as a possible solution to the problem and as they went from house to house it was hoped that they would act as a link between the vicar and his parishioners and stimulate the latter into attending church. In the Church of England a scheme of this type had been started as early as 1812, when Daniel Wilson founded a District Visiting Society at St. John's, Islington. Bishop Sumner of Chester was convinced of the value of lay visiting and Bishop Davys of Peterborough thought that it might bring rich and poor together, though it seems not to have had this effect and at times and in places it came to have a forbidding inquisitorial character. At Kenwyn-cum-Kea in Cornwall in the 1850s each visitor was given twenty-one houses to visit. The visitors were provided with forms on which they were to enter the details of each household. The names, the occupation, the number and the religous body to which the inhabitants belonged were to be recorded and the visited were to be asked if they could read, if they had a Bible and if they were communicants. The vicar wanted to know also if the children had been baptised and were at school. There might be a fortnightly or monthly meeting of the visitors of a parish with their vicar and needless to say the employment of young ladies in this capacity had to be very carefully supervised.

In the very small parish, on the other hand, there was no need to go visiting for the incumbent saw the whole of his flock almost every day. The rector of Fishley, near Acle Bridge in Norfolk, who died in 1904 having held the living for twenty years, had a parish of eighteen people, which included the rectory household.[5]

When the parochial clergy went visiting down grimy streets or lanes fringed with cow parsley, they went not only as spiritual persons but also as the bringers of social relief, and this dual function could very easily render their visits nugatory as far as they were concerned. It was difficult to turn the minds of parishioners towards prayer when they were hoping for a shilling, for some clergy when they went visiting filled their pockets with shillings and distributed them as they went to those that they thought were in special need. This naturally tempted the visited to spin tales of woe and cottage women, when they discovered this source of income, quickly adapted themselves to tapping it, so that incumbents on their rounds would find a whole population plunged in misery and afflicted with incredible troubles. When Blomfield went visiting in Bishopsgate as rector, he thought he noticed the same children in the different rooms of the tenements and discovered that they were let down from the window from one storey to another so that families might appear larger than they were. It was difficult to judge rightly when money should be given and when not, and it did not seem that the giving of alms brought more to church; but, on the other hand, relief was sometimes given by the clergy when it was needed and many of the poor had reason to be grateful for the visit of their vicar. Charlotte Brontë describes in *Shirley* the visit of Mr. Hall, the vicar of Nunnely, to the Farrens, where the husband is out of work, and catches the blend of social welfare and spiritual concern which many of the clergy combined in their visiting. Mr. Hall speaks to Mrs. Farren of the possibility of a loan:

> 'Well, I'll speak to one or two friends, and I think I can promise to let him have five pounds in a day or two: as a loan, ye mind, not a gift: he must pay it back.'

'I understand, sir: I'm quite agreeable to that.'

'Meantime, there's a few shillings for you, Grace, just to keep the pot boiling till custom comes. Now, bairns, stand up in a row and say your catechism, while your mother goes and buys some dinner: for you've not had much today, I'll be bound. You begin, Ben. What is your name?'

Mr. Hall stayed till Grace came back; then he hastily took his leave, shaking hands with both Farren and his wife: just at the door, he said to them a few brief but very earnest words of religious consolation and exhortation: with a mutual 'God bless you, sir!'

'God bless you, my friends!' they separated.

In spite of all the difficulties, then, many vicars and rectors and curates found visiting worthwhile and spent many hours upon it. Twelve houses a day should be visited, one authority recommended; and an active priest in a large town parish ought not to be content with less than thirty-six to forty visits weekly. It should be possible to visit the whole of a country parish with three hundred families in six weeks, making allowance for the fact that some of them would need visiting more than once in that time. When Bishop Stubbs was at Chester he thought it easy for a clergyman to know every one of his flock in a parish of one thousand, and even a parish of four thousand might be handled by a single priest in the same way. 'Your grand occupation lies out of doors and among your own people,' R. W. Evans told his readers, and Canon Newbolt quoted with approval the German proverb, 'The best soil for the field is that in the farmer's shoe'. In spite of his experience at Bishopsgate, Blomfield told the clergy of the diocese of London that house-to-house visitation was the secret of their usefulness.

So the clergy would walk and ride for miles around their parishes, visiting their parishioners. In his younger days at Danby-in-Cleveland in Yorkshire, J. C. Atkinson seldom walked less than thirty-five or forty miles a week going to church or from house to house and estimated that in the forty years and more he had been vicar of the parish he had walked over seventy thousand miles in the course of his clerical work alone. Others had horses. 'What would a parson of a large country parish do without a horse!' Armstrong exclaimed at East Dereham, 'went to Dillington, two miles off, to baptise a child; to Badley Moor, two miles on the other side of the town to give Holy Communion to eight poor people. Then Toftwood Common, a mile further, to see a sick person. Stayed to give Communion to another person near the town and sent the phaeton home. This would have taken three days to do if walking.'[6] A year later the horse went berserk, was sold and put to the plough; Armstrong thought it would do him good. Complaints were made at times by clergymen who could not afford a horse, and the vicar of Fenwick in Yorkshire regretted in 1865 that he could not visit his scattered parishioners in winter without one, yet on sixty pounds a year could not afford to buy one. At the end of the century bicycles began to offer a cheaper and easier form of transport than the horse for clerical visiting, though at the same time they made it cheaper and easier for parishioners to get out of their parishes, so that the cycling vicar might find no one at home when he called.

In visiting the parochial clergy came up against dissent, which varied in its strength from parish to parish. Armstrong completed a visitation of a hundred families in the outlying parts of his parish in 1852 and noted that thirteen families were dissenters, two families were without Bibles, fourteen children were unbaptised and only fifteen had ever received Holy Communion. Four years later he wrote, 'I mounted my horse and visited poor Dack near Cressenhall bridge, a dying free-thinker. Thence, by cross-roads to Northall Green to expostulate with young Mrs. Jones on turning Mormonite.' R. W. Evans found a good deal of dissent in Westmorland and described what he might find when he set out for a hamlet in his parish set deep in the country, the inhabitants of which were not by any means pillars of the Anglican establishment. At the first house there was a family that never went to church, who pleaded that they could go to chapel or say their prayers at home; they should be told that these were no possible alternatives to the services of the Church of England. At the second house there were dissenters, who practised occasional conformity by appearing from time to time at the parish church. Evans did not think that much could be done with them and only the example of the clergyman's unremitting industry might bring them in. At the third house there was a man who went to church occasionally but was, alas, free and easy in his living, who was a slippery customer indeed, always dodging clerical remonstrance, for should he be reminded that families who did not call upon the Lord might become extinct and desolate, he would reply with an anecdote on the extinction of an old family in the neighbourhood. Nor was the inhabitant of the next house any more satisfactory, for here was a widower with a comfortable annuity who spent his time over the daily papers and was the oracle of the village gossips. Once he had been to hear exciting preachers but, knowing his Bible, often found the preachers to be wrong; disillusioned, therefore, he had turned to the cheap periodicals of the day, and did not go to church, believing everybody to be the same. A bitter and irreconcilable opponent of religion and the Church lived behind the next front door, but he should be visited nevertheless, as should the person next door who led a careless life and was possibly a drunkard. Only in the last house of all did there appear to be any response to the vicar's visit for it contained a desolate widow. She was to be comforted by having read to her an apposite but not very obvious portion of Scripture, which should then be expounded and taken as a basis of prayer. So the hamlet was visited from door to door and the vicar on his way home might well reflect on the waywardness of human nature and the irreligion of the people. At night he should pray over the events of the day.[7]

That the house-going parson made a church-going people was an aphorism often quoted by the advisers of the Victorian clergy, but if Evans's experience was anything to go by it did not appear to be true. The house-going parson, however, might take the Church to the people in the form of cottage lectures, held in houses in the outlying parts of a parish, where twenty or thirty people would cram into a small room with windows and doors tightly shut, which George Eliot described as producing an atmosphere impregnated with spring flowers and perspiration. They were held on weekdays in town and country and proved to be immensely popular. In a London parish a vicar borrowed a room, paid a shilling a night for light and fire and, with a few forms, three or four dips, a table and some cards of hymns especially printed for the occasion, found that he had all that was needed. The lectures were often crowded.[8] The holding of a lecture in the country on a dark night could be hazardous, as Kilvert discovered in the New Year of 1878:

At 6.15 I took Arthur's lantern and went up to Crafta Webb to give a cottage lecture at Eliza Preece's house. It was pitch dark and raining, the road very steep and bad, and before I got to the end of my journey I was streaming with perspiration, and wet without and within. Just before I reached Eliza Preece's cottage the paraffin lamp in the lantern went out and left me in the dark so that I had much ado and worried myself to find the garden gate. The room was full of people, there was a cheerful fire, and a lamp bright on the table, and I was glad I had come, for the people seemed glad to see me. I had a hymn first, 'Sun of my soul' then some of the Evening Prayer, and read Hebrews xi, 8, 9, 10 and spoke of our going into the year 1878 as Abraham went out at the call of God into the strange and Promised Land. Just before I ended poor Mrs. Jenkins fainted and had to be carried to the door to be revived with fresh air and cold water. She had been turned suddenly out of Bredwardine Bridge Gate house and been obliged to move to a damp, long untenanted cottage, which had troubled her much and made her weak and ill. She was violently sick and then better and some of the kind neighbours helped her home. The incident distressed us all and brought our little gathering to a sudden close.[9]

The fainting and sickness of poor Mrs. Jenkins serves as a reminder that there was a great deal of illness about in the nineteenth century, for much of which there was no known cure. The death rate had fallen dramatically in the eighty years after 1730, but was then checked in spite of the constant advance in medicine, largely due to the appalling conditions in the slums of the great towns and cities; and it was only in the 1870s and later that the rate began to decline again as the Victorians began to tackle the sanitation and lighting of these great urban areas. To the many sick and dying of the period the clergy were called upon to minister, for the duty to do so was specifically laid upon them by the Prayer Book, which provided a service for the visitation of the sick; and it was generally agreed that though there might be doubts about the advisability of the frequent visiting of the healthy, the visiting of the sick was one of their more important tasks. Not all the clergy, however, undertook this duty. A friend of Ashton Oxenden's appointed to a living in Wiltshire in 1840 found that the very old previous incumbent held no service on wet Sundays, had not administered the Holy Communion for eighteen months, and that when a sick person wanted a visit would send a shilling saying that that would do more good for him than his prayers.

Yet the diaries of the period show that clergy resident in their parishes did visit the sick, sometimes in appalling conditions. At Wath the rector went to see a woman in 1816 who insisted on prayers being read, though she could not hear a word, and the day after he administered to her the sacrament. He noted also that he was taking up his potatoes. A few months later he gave the sacrament to another parishioner who was not likely to live for more than forty-eight hours, visited him again three days later and again four days after that, having sowed in the meantime his mangel-wurzels and carrots. John Skinner at Camerton visited an old man at the public house, who slept in a hayloft reached by mounting a ladder from the outside, the floor of which was dangerous and made of hurdles which were nearly rotten. Later he learnt that boys and drunken colliers had driven him from the place and that he had died near the coke pit. Kingsley visited a man sick with fever, lying in a little fetid ground-floor bedroom and, before saying a word, rushed up the stairs with a large auger with which he bored several holes above the bed's head for ventilation, to the great astonishment of the inhabitants. Kilvert took the sacrament to a sick man and afterwards described the setting:

> What a scene it was, the one small room up in the roof of the hovel, almost dark, in which I could not stand upright, the shattered window, almost empty of glass, the squalid bed, the close horrid smell, the continual crying and wailing of the children below, the pattering of the rain on the tiles close overhead, the ceaseless moaning of the sick man with his face bound about with a napkin. 'Lord have mercy, Lord have mercy upon me' he moaned. I was almost exhausted crouching down at the little dirty window to catch the light of the gloomy rainy afternoon.[10]

Heights of horror were reached when typhoid or cholera swept through the multitudes living in the grimy, crowded, insanitary tenements of the slums. Cholera in Britain was a nineteenth-century terror, its symptoms frightening, its cause for many years unknown, its treatment ineffective. It began often with giddiness, ringing in the ears and a feeling of uneasiness and anxiety, usually followed by a tremendous evacuation of the bowels when the whole intestines seemed to be emptied at once. There might then be felt a fluttering in the pit of the stomach and a sense of weight or constriction around the waist, succeeded by a prickly sensation in the arms and legs, sometimes extending to the fingers and the toes. Hands and feet became clammy and there was often a pain in the forehead; movement brought sickness or purging. The odourless rice-water motions, which actually consisted of tiny fragments of the lining of the intestines, were the classic diagnostic sign and often the body lost several pints of fluid in a few minutes, expelled as if from a syringe, leaving the patient's bed-clothes saturated, the floor awash and the patient shrunken and shrivelled. Cramps followed in the second stage of the disease; acute pains in fingers or toes, spreading up the limbs and across the chest, were often accompanied by pain in the stomach, and the skin might turn blue or black. Breathing became difficult, and the air from the mouth might issue with a low moaning or whistling sound. The cramps might last several hours, making the patient feel that he was being bored through with a screw, and might lead to contractions so violent that the body was rolled almost into a ball, which could not be straightened out till after death. Even at that stage he might still recover, but if not he would linger for two or three hours or maybe a week or longer, during which time he would lie inert with eyes turned upward and though conscious, would appear not to hear what was said to him, though occasionally he might reply in a feeble, plaintive whisper. The brain appeared to be unimpaired, though there seemed to be no understanding of the situation and no fear of dying. From this point it was but a short step to coma and death.[11]

Many agreed that cleanliness was helpful in combatting the disease, since it struck in the dirtiest parts of the towns, but the cause of it was for a long time unknown. Veal, smoked meat, salted fish, gravies, cucumbers and cheese were under suspicion, while some believed that it was contagious, and others were miasmatists, who thought that it came from some evil force floating in the air, perhaps from heaps of refuse, stagnant water, a change in temperature or barometric pressure, wind or thunderstorms. Flies were criticised and the water supply was suspected. With so many possible causes being suggested it is not surprising that many forms of treatment were being advocated, ranging from the taking of calomel and opium to the wearing of a wide belt of thick, warm material around the stomach. The application of heat in the form of hot blankets, bags full of hot sand, and pillow-slips containing hot bran and sulphur had its advocates; and on the other hand there were those who advised the application of ice. In the 1850s a doctor pointed to water as the source of the disease, but even in the London epidemic of 1866, when evidence that this was indeed the cause became available, there were still those who held other views; and it was not until

1884 that the cholera germ, a short, thick, curved organism resembling a comma, was discovered. The last cholera epidemic in Great Britain was in the years 1892 and 1893.

In the first epidemic at Sunderland in 1831 one clergyman was found praying outside the door of a sick-room, but no other case of cowardice on the part of doctors or clergy was reported and in other places they stood naturally in the forefront of the battle. When cholera reached Bilston in 1832 the Rev. William Leigh set up a Board of Health with himself at its head, equipped as a cholera hospital a former barracks, hired a nurse and an ambulance, distributed free lime for the whitewashing of houses, mobilised cleaners to scrub out premises from which a patient had been removed and warned the population, by poster and handbill, to seek advice when the disease first appeared. He went to Birmingham and returned with cartloads of coffins, which were piled in the yard of the hospital, and founded a school for the orphans of cholera victims, making it a rule that the children, of whatever denomination, should attend the parish church every Sunday morning. Seven hundred and fifty died of cholera at Bilston. In London in 1849 the Rev. James Gillman, vicar of Holy Trinity, Lambeth, did not go home for three weeks for fear of taking the cholera with him, but slept on the sofa in the surgery of the parish doctor. He started a very cheap life insurance scheme, which prospered and blossomed into the Prudential Assurance Company.[12]

The clergy faced heart-rending tragedies when the cholera struck, for whole families might be wiped out, or all the children taken and their parents left, or the parents only taken and the children orphaned. At St. George's Mission, in the parish of St. George's-in-the-East, London, Charles Lowder told how two of the children in the Mission had an elder sister, about eighteen years old, who was first taken and removed to the cholera ward where she died. Then,

> a younger one, well and fresh on the Sunday—indeed after the service in Church coming up with her usual childish affection to one of the Mission Clergy, who passed near her

mother's house, to tell of her sister's illness—was taken ill
herself on the Tuesday, and removed to the same ward as
that in which her sister died. The mother was following the
elder one to the grave when the youngest was taken ill and
laid on her bed at home, when the same Priest, called in by a
neighbour, felt it his duty to carry her off in his arms to the
ward. Here she was laid in the next bed to her sister, and yet
both so ill that for a long time they were unconscious of
each other's nearness, and on those beds both died, the
elder one just able to say the Lord's Prayer with the
Priest.[13]

The effects of cholera and typhoid were desperately tragic,
but there were many other diseases, such as consumption,
which caused havoc when they struck and might bring much
pain to their victims who could only find partial relief with
medicines. It was the duty of the vicar then to go to the sick-
room and to say prayers at the bedside, for which eventuality
the Prayer Book had thoughtfully provided a special order of
service. The visitation of the sick was a sombre offering,
beginning with the minister of the parish kneeling down and
praying 'Remember not, Lord, out iniquities, nor the iniquities of our forefathers: spare us, good Lord, spare thy people, who thou hast redeemed with thy most precious blood,
and be not angry with us for ever'; and through the service
sickness was regarded as predominantly a punishment for sin,
a whip for the wilful who disobeyed God's laws, though it was
also possible to think of it as providing an opportunity of dis-
playing patience in adversity and of strengthening a man's
faith. Some thought, therefore, that the use of the service in
its entirety was inadvisable, while others believed that if it
were used once it were better not to use it again. A few
thought it the most beautiful service in the Prayer Book and
the changes made in it between 1549 and 1662 entirely for
the better.

These changes had eliminated Unction but had not
abolished the possibility of private confession to a priest if the
sick person had his conscience troubled with any weighty mat-

ter; nor was private confession entirely confined to the sick, for the Prayer Book allowed it to those who wished to come to the communion yet were troubled in mind. The Tractarians, therefore, could use this evidence as a bridgehead from which to extend the practice of confession in their parishes and elsewhere so that it became a regular part of their ministry. Newman in his Anglican days said that confession was the life of the parochial charge and that without it all was hollow; and Keble thought their one great grievance was its neglect. Yet slowly it became established on a regular basis in some parishes, though not without opposition, led by the Queen, who disliked it. 'She thinks,' she wrote to Dean Stanley, 'a *complete Reformation* is what we want. But if *that* is *impossible*, the archbishop should have the *power* given him, by *Parliament*, to *stop all* these ritualistic practices, dressings, bowings, etc., and everything of that kind, and *above all*, *all* attempts at *confession*.' Lord Shaftesbury concurred and was reported to have said 'if the rubrics allow it—well then, away with the rubrics'.

But it was impossible to change the Prayer Book rubrics without tearing apart much of the fabric of the Church of England, so the rubrics remained and confessions continued. Incumbents with their freeholds could not be removed for hearing confessions, though a couple of curates were accused in 1858 of asking improper questions in the confessional and one of them had his licence withdrawn by the Bishop of London, without reason given. The other, however, who served at the vast, dark church of All Saints, Boyne Hill, Maidenhead, was cleared of the charge against him and by the 1860s a few churches had begun to advertise on church notice boards the hours at which confessions could be heard.

Less controversial was the duty of the minister in the sickroom to urge the sick person to repent of his sins, without making a formal confession, before he went to meet his Maker. This required a nice sense of judgment, for the strength of the spiritual depth charge to be placed under the sick man's bed must be sufficient to shake him but not to shatter him. Too great an inquisition on the patient's sins might lead to the door being barred against the minister when he came again; and the story was told of a woman in Manchester who, on receiving a clergyman, broke out with, 'Eh minister, I'se got liberty, I'se got the blessing.' 'Very well, Mary, but can you tell me who the Lord Jesus Christ is?' 'Nay, mon!' 'Can you tell me why Jesus Christ died on the Cross?' 'Nay, mon, I'm no schollard.' 'Well, Mary, the Lord Jesus Christ is the Son of God, and He died on the Cross to save sinners— have you any sins?' 'Eh! mon! but thee'd better be getting doon stairs; I doon't like thee talk!'[14] The sick could be wily, priests were advised to note. They might be compliant and agree with all that was said, or they might be reserved and say little or nothing, or they might talk a great deal. They might be fanatical in their belief that their sins were already forgiven, or they might be thoroughly hardened characters. Sadly, it was necessary to doubt the sincerity of the repentance of the very sick, for Evans had seen how those who had recovered did not in fact live up to their vows and resolutions. It was necessary, therefore, to continue to visit the convalescent.[15]

The Prayer Book also charged the priest with the duty of admonishing the sick person to make his will if he had not already done so, and 'to declare his debts, what he oweth, and what is owing unto him; for the better discharging of his conscience, and the quietness of his Executors.' The sick were to be urged also to be liberal to the poor in the disposition of their effects, though presumably the poor themselves escaped being given this advice. The Last Will and Testament, like the Old and New Testaments, had a place in the sick-room, and the clergy were to concern themselves with legacies as well as with the law and love of God.

Provision had been especially made in the *Book of Common Prayer* for the sick to receive communion. There should be two or three present when this occurred, but if parishioners refused to come, then the minister must go alone, taking with him a surplice, with a chalice and paten of a good size. A silver egg-cup was frowned upon. At all times the priest should be careful in cases of possible infection and must not rush into danger even if, on the other hand, he was not to shrink from it.

In extreme cases he was advised to take a biscuit and a glass of wine before entering the sick-room where, once admitted, he was not to stand between the patient and the fire where the air was drawn from the former to the latter. He was to avoid inhaling the patient's breath, should not attempt to hold the patient's hand, and on leaving should ventilate his clothes. In the sick room he should be more like a breeze than a tornado. A hearty clergyman striding about the muddy lanes of his parish with thick boots and the strongest of legs, shouting across the fields, might enter a sick-room bringing with him an exuberance of vitality which would act like a tonic on the sick. But on the other hand it might be almost insufferable. It was better to be gentle, to tread noiselessly, to speak softly and be brief.

The clergy and their wives were not above doctoring their parishioners when they were sick, though they might not venture to treat the more serious illnesses. At Wath the rector noted in his diary that on one Saturday in 1817 he had vaccinated three or four, thus helping to keep the smallpox at bay which had been such a scourge in previous centuries. Sydney Smith in his parish at Combe Florey, near Taunton, had an apothecary's shop in which he kept drugs and groceries and was delighted when half the parish went down with influenza as it improved his medical practice; but scarlet fever, which brought fifteen deaths, was beyond him. 'You will naturally suppose that I have killed all these people,' he wrote, 'by doctoring them: but scarlet fever awes me and is above my aim. I leave it to the professional and graduated homicides.' When diptheria appeared in the neighbourhood of Eversley in 1857 and proved to be very fatal, Kingsley went in and out of the cottages with great bottles of gargle under his arm. At Stanford-in-the-Vale the parish doctor looked after thirteen parishes and called all the men John and all the women Mary; Christopher Wordsworth maintained that the kitchen physic of his wife was quite as beneficial to the patients as anything that the doctor could provide. At Watling in Sussex E. B. Ellman doctored the people free.

Towards the end of the century, as medical science

advanced and the medical profession became more highly qualified, the clergy ceased to practise amateur medicine on their parishioners and contented themselves with more spiritual ministrations, though they could still be sent for to help in matters like the death of a pet, or arrears of rent, or the spitefulness of a neighbour. Vicars were still visiting when Victoria died and were still numerous enough to reach a large part of the population, especially in the country, in this way.

NOTES

1 G. K. A. Bell, *Randall Davidson*, Vol. 1., pp. 89–90.
2 H. Alford, *Life, Journals and Letters*, p. 488.
3 B. A. Smith, *Dean Church*, p. 131.
4 R. M. Grier, *John Allen*, p. 302.
5 F. R. Barry, *Period of My Life*, p. 159.
6 B. J. Armstrong, *Armstrong's Norfolk Diary*, p. 119.
7 R. W. Evans, *The Bishopric of Souls*, p. 64.
8 C. H. Simpkinson, *Bishop Thorold*, pp. 30–1.
9 Francis Kilvert, *Diary*, January 3rd, 1878.
10 Ibid., October 7th, 1870.
11 Norman Longmate, *King Cholera*, pp. 17–19.
12 Ibid., pp. 110–15, 171.
13 C. F. Lowder, *Twenty-One Years in St. George's Mission*, p. 110.
14 Herbert James, *The Country Clergyman and his Work*, p. 96.
15 R. W. Evans, *op. cit.*, pp. 68–87.

CHAPTER'8

Schools

WHEN JOHN SKINNER found an obscenity written on the wall of the church porch at Camerton in 1830, he confided to his diary that it would be better for the lower orders to know nothing about writing if they were going to produce such fruits as these. There was a good deal of education being conducted in his parish at the time, for two years earlier he had noted what was available for the population of upwards of a thousand, listing six schools and the numbers of their pupils:

At Mrs. Jarrett's School	62 (girls)
Girls at Mrs. Sellers	20
Mrs. Moon	16
Mrs. Maggs (30 boys, 20 girls)	50
The Woman in Edgill's Building, Cridlingcot	7
Job Edwards	12
	167

The four last schools were for small children and there was a great need for a school for boys.

At the lowest end of the educational ladder were the dame schools, carried on in cottage rooms where younger children up to the age of six or seven were taught. They varied enormously in their quality, depending on the dame, but some must have been very good for Thomas Cooper, the Chartist, described how he attended one in the larger, lower room of a dame's two-storied cottage, which was always full and where the arts of reading and spelling were expertly and laboriously taught. Cooper soon became her favourite scholar and could read the tenth chapter of Nehemiah, with all its hard names, 'like the parson in church'—as she used to say—and could spell wondrously. J. C. Hare told the clergy of the arch-deaconry of Lewes that he thought it better to leave the younger children in these schools, which were to be found in nearly every hamlet, and that he would regret their extinction. At Watling in Sussex, E. B. Ellman established six of them in various parts of the parish and visited them twice a week in order to give religious instruction. They proved to have a great deal of life in them, being easily opened and shut and moved from one cottage to another, so that as late as 1872 there were two hundred and forty of them in Greenwich, kept in back rooms or basements.

Some, however, wanted a properly built and supervised infant school. At Wymeswold one was completed in 1839, and, proving more costly than had been anticipated, necessitated the holding of a bazaar on a large scale in order to clear the debt. They were not always well attended, for at St. Peter's, Derby, one morning there were twenty-six present in a room that could hold two hundred. A delightful feature of this schoolroom was a large bed at the bottom of the room, equipped with mattress and sheet, where the little ones were laid to rest if they became sleepy; and this was often provided in Derbyshire schools.[1] In the infant schools children should be taught to read, to form habits of decorum, order and cleanliness and to learn to love truth, gentleness and obedience; while lying, thieving and bad language were to be scrupulously discouraged. Women only should teach in them and several small schools were preferred to one that was larger.

But the schools which absorbed most of the energies of vicars and rectors were those for boys and girls between the ages of seven and fourteen, though unfortunately the Poor Law of 1834 caused the boys to leave at eleven or twelve because their families needed all the wages that they could get, a result criticized by one archdeacon as moral and spiritual infanticide. In the erection of a school for this age group the incumbent would usually play a leading part, cajoling the local squire into giving the land on which it was to be built and encouraging subscriptions from far and near towards the building, to which he would contribute generously himself. Bishop Fraser of Manchester asserted that but for the zeal and activity of the clergy and their large sacrifices of money, labour and time, in three-quarters of the rural parishes of England there would be no school or at best only the semblance of one. A school, then, was most likely built by a vicar, who was advised to site it near the parsonage so that he could call in at any time if he had ten minutes to spare, for a school was the parish priest's right hand, to be treated as the vestibule of the church. The children most certainly were to be made to go to church on Sundays or otherwise they would be found bird's-nesting or getting nuts.

There were cases where the vicar did not have it all his own way at the school and especially this was so when the squire had not only given the land on which it stood, but had paid for the building and had undertaken to find the salary of the teacher. Sir John Boileau, who had done all these things at Ketteringham, refused to permit the schoolroom to be used without his sanction, allowed its use for confirmation instruction but not for missionary meetings, and was doubtful whether he would allow it to be occupied for lectures on the Scriptures if strangers from other parishes came. It was his school.

A few schools refused all help from outside and were self-sufficient, though even they might be visited by diocesan inspectors. As late as 1867, however, some schools were still not inspected for there was the fear that inspectors would interfere in the running of the school, though their duty was to furnish information and offer practical advice. But most of the clergy found that they could not build or run a school without help from outside, which was indeed available but came with strings attached so that the vicar's authority was a little circumscribed. The chief agency in the field as far as the Church of England was concerned was the National Society, founded in 1811 to give to the poor such knowledge and habits as would be sufficient to guide them through their life in their proper stations, and especially 'to teach them the doctrine of Religion according to the principles of the Established Church, and to train them to the performance of their religious duties by an early discipline'. It made grants, but on conditions. It required evidence that the school was locally supported, that it could be opened free of debt and that the land on which it stood was freehold or else held on a long lease. It appointed inspectors and made building regulations. The schools it supported were often called National Schools.[2]

Then, in 1833, the government set aside twenty thousand pounds for education, to be administered by the Treasury through the National Society and the British and Foreign School Society, which was the nonconformist equivalent of the Anglican body, and State participation in education had begun. The money, given annually, and raised to one hundred thousand pounds in 1846, was used for the building of schools, especially in the large towns, but with the increasing involvement of the State there came naturally enough an increasing demand for State inspection. In 1840 agreement had been reached between Church and State over the inspection of schools by which the Privy Council formally appointed and dismissed inspectors, but the Church nominated them and terminated their appointment in church schools; and then, in 1858, the government decided to measure out its grants according to the standard reached in reading, writing and arithmetic, which for many years was the system used until in 1890 it was modified and relaxed. Vicars in control of schools, therefore, had to make sure that their teachers were able to teach competently the three R's and the day when the children were examined in them was a fearful one. Flora Thompson gives a picture of such an inspection from a child's point of view, where the inspector, who turned out to be a little elderly clergyman, with an immense paunch and an apparent hatred of children, made them write letters to their grandmothers describing imaginary school holidays and once dictated to them two verses of 'The Ancient Mariner.'

But first the school had to be built. The National Society suggested in 1876 that it should have seven square feet of floor space per child, high windows and, if the ceiling were flat, apertures to allow the escape of foul air. Nine years later it wanted the minimum height of a classroom to be ten feet and the ceiling not flat, while a vicar thought a distance of twelve to fourteen feet from the floor to the wall plate was necessary, and the windows high so that the children could not be distracted by passing objects. When curate at Eversley, Kingsley would go to the school every day and teach as long as he could stand the heat and smell, so the height of the classroom, open to the roof, was dictated largely by the need for air and ventilation since the children were by no means always clean. It was recommended, also, that when school was over the windows of the schoolroom should be immediately opened, both in summer and winter. Cleanliness was not forgotten, however, for a tank should be built to collect the rainwater from the roof, and there should be W.C.s, each furnished with a wooden trough, lined in lead, extending the whole length of each closet and having three or four inches of water constantly lying in it, which should be run off once a day.[3]

A playground was of immense value, for without one the children would play in the street. It should be walled round and on a very gentle slope so that the water would flow off it freely after a shower; it should be laid with pit or river gravel. The sides of the playground, it was surprisingly suggested, should be planted with small fruit bushes such as red and blackcurrants, together with a few patches of strawberries; and there should be flowers and shrubs. All of these, being constantly in sight and within reach, meant the exercise of the virtues of honesty and self-denial on the part of the children.

Once built, the running of the school was most likely to be in the hands of the incumbent. The National Society's annual report for 1840 said that the government of schools in country parishes was often entirely in the hands of clergymen and that in many places there was not a single individual outside his family who had the will and opportunity to render assistance. Seven years later their powers were a little clipped by the need to have a management committee for each church school, though the vicar was to be the chairman of the committee and to superintend the religious instruction that was given. In all other respects the committee was to govern the school and appoint the teachers, but nevertheless the incumbent had a commanding role and it was usually the case that where there was an able vicar there was an efficient school and where there was an inefficient vicar there was a poor one. At King's Somborne in Hampshire, the vicar graduated the scale of fees according to the parents' means so that the farmer paid more than the labourer. The teaching was attractive and the curriculum liberal, for the children's surroundings were used as a starting point for the teaching of everyday science, in which the vicar himself took a part, with the consequence that the number of children and the income grew in a most satisfactory manner and the school was praised by the Committee of the Privy Council on Education. On the other hand, at Upper Sapey in Herefordshire the school account was always overdrawn and the teacher always changing.

It was difficult to inveigle subscriptions for schools from the wealthier parishioners. R. W. Evans noticed shopkeepers and farmers found them less romantic and were less willing to support them than the missionary work to which they were also asked to contribute. 'The poor schoolmaster with his ferule, ruler, desk, copybooks and boys, cannot compare with the barbaric chieftain with his gold and his throne, and his soldiers and his wives.'[4] Schools, therefore, were run on a shoestring and because teachers were often poorly paid they were often of poor quality or, if they were competent, did not stay long in one place but moved on to more remunerative pastures. The situation grew worse for church schools after 1870, when board schools arrived on the scene and paid more to teachers than their Anglican counterparts; an inquiry in Worcester in 1887 revealed that in Church of England schools the masters were being paid one hundred and twenty pounds a year while in board schools they were getting one hundred and forty-eight pounds, and mistresses in Church of England schools were receiving seventy pounds a year while in board schools the salary was one hundred and one pounds. When J. C. Atkinson went to Danby in Yorkshire and wondered why the schoolmaster was incompetent, he received the reply, 'Wheea, he could dee nought else. He had muddled away his land, and we put him in scheealmaster that he mou't get a bite of bread'. Morwenstow was astonished to find a man called Trood appointed as teacher in its school who had been a slave-driver in the West Indies and had returned home with a mulatto wife.

There was a great gulf fixed between the vicar and the schoolteacher, which lasted throughout the century though it lessened towards the end. It was caused partly by a difference in education, partly by a difference in income, and partly by a difference of status in the eyes of the world, which made the vicar immeasurably superior to the teacher or teachers in the school. An inspector of schools in England and Wales, who did not confine himself to inspecting schools which received grants from the government, wished that the different classes might be more brought together, but although he had met several instances of a schoolmistress being received at a clergyman's table, he could scarcely recollect an instance out of London, with the exception of the Dean of Bangor, where a clergyman shook hands with, or even talked familiarly with, a parochial schoolmaster. At Wantage, Butler received all the school staff at twelve forty-five p.m. on a Saturday in order to hear their report on the week's work and those teachers who had been trained in his own schools always addressed him as 'sir'. He deemed this to be due to the vicar of the parish and considered equality and familiarity out of keeping with the Fifth Commandment. Social pretensions on the part of a teacher could be quickly squashed, as they were when a school treat, which Flora Thompson witnessed as a child, was held at the Manor House in her parish, and her teacher went to the front door for tea in the drawing-room, something that had not been done before. She did indeed have tea in the drawing-room, but in a few minutes was back in the servants' hall murmuring to one of her monitors, 'Dear Mrs. Bracewell gave me my tea first, because, as she said, she knew I was anxious to get back to my children.'

The teachers' first duty was to give to the children knowledge of the three R's, leaving what church schools regarded as the most significant subject of all, religious instruction, in the hands of the vicar. It was generally agreed that the Bible was unsuitable as a classbook for learning to read, since it associated the Scriptures with the drudgery of acquiring this art in the minds of the young. In reading, grammar should not be neglected, nor the etymology of words. The dissection of a word like 'unprecedented' could be undertaken with profit, for it could lead first to other words beginning with 'un', such as uncommon and uncivil, and then to other syllables at the beginning of words which also signified 'not', which would lead to ignorant, illiterate, immortal, irregular, disjointed, atheist and nonconformist. Future ploughboys, having acquired this vocabulary, could then proceed to the syllable 'pre' in unprecedented and learning the meaning of previous, premature and prelude. And then 'cede' would follow. Writing entailed the copying of copperplate maxims such as 'count ten before you speak', imitated laboriously with pot-hooks and hangers, copied with tongue hanging out, but leading to legibility when letters had to be written in later life. The introduction of steel pens for this was advocated in large schools as a great saver of time. The four simple rules of arithmetic, addition to division were to be instilled into every child, however humble his condition or prospects; when able to add he should be given shop-bills and accounts of one kind or another on which to exercise his skill.

Geography might be usefully included in the curriculum, particularly because the thoughts of so many of the working classes were turning to emigration, making it desirable that the poor, who were to be given the Kingdom of Heaven, should know something also about the earth. A good globe might prove too expensive to purchase, though a benefactor might be disposed to give one, but large school maps could be had at moderate prices which, hung on the walls, almost insensibly conveyed an idea of the subject as well as brightening the schoolroom; one school at least had splendid maps, but no lessons in geography. Industrial drawing was important, though regrettably it was attempted in few parochial schools. Singing was to be encouraged, since schools were the nurseries of church choirs, and Archdeacon Hare had heard that it was of great benefit in a penitentiary in Paris for vagabond boys, softening the heart and unfolding the understanding. It was desirable, therefore, that children should be taught to sing. Needlework could be given to the girls and the boys might be encouraged in handicraft, which would help the school to meet its expenses, give the children a trifling reward and teach them perseverance and industry; and more adventurous teachers might include history and nature study as well.

These subjects, however, were dwarfed by the giant of religious instruction, which the clergy themselves were urged to give assiduously and frequently in their schools. They should go two or three times a week, preferably on Mondays and Thursdays, for on Mondays they could examine the children in their memory of the church services the previous day and on Thursdays they were not themselves yet busy with preparations for the Sunday that was to follow. An hour a week was the minimum time that should be given to this work, and an hour a day the maximum. The Bible, the Prayer Book and the catechism were to be the sources of their teaching and it was suggested that by the time the children left school they were to have, among other things, a clear knowledge of Genesis, the life of Jesus and the early chapters of the Acts of the Apostles. These they might acquire, along with much else, by learning religious alphabets, like the simple one sung to the tune of 'O come, all ye faithful', which began:

> A—is for Angel—who praises the Lord;
> B—is for Bible—God's most Holy Word;
> C—is for Church—where the righteous resort;

D—is for Devil—who wishes our hurt.

or they might learn a more advanced Biblical example, taking in some geography on the way:

G—is for Goschen—a rich and good land;
H—is for Horeb—where Moses did stand;
I—is for Italy—where Rome stands so fair;
J—is for Joppa—and Peter lived there;
K—is for Kadish—where Miriam died;
L—is for Lebanon—can't be denied.[5]

The clergy were urged to remember the exceeding ignorance of the labouring poor, to use pictures in their teaching and to make the children learn the psalms, collects and Sunday gospels, but inevitably the knowledge was not always accurately taken in. Kilvert received as an answer to the question, 'What happened on Palm Sunday?' the reply, 'Jesus Christ went up to heaven on an ass.' Another time a boy, when asked what makes a true sacrament, wrote, 'It is a burnt offering, sometimes it is a ram and sometimes it is a bullock. There was a man named Elisha and he had a son and the Lord said to him, "Take thy son and kill it". That is a sackrement.' A curate at West Firle in Sussex became involved with children in the discussion of miracles, which no one seemed able to describe, so he said to them, 'Suppose you were to wake up and saw the sun shining in the middle of the night what would you say it was?' 'Full moon.' 'But supposing someone told you it was the sun and not the full moon. What would you say then?' 'It's a lie.' 'I don't tell lies, if I told you . . .' 'Ye be drunk.' The same curate when he became a vicar, found his children singing 'Wild shepherds watched their flocks by night' in spite of frequent correction, and whey they were asked what the shepherds were doing, the answer was 'Drinking', for they could not imagine men sitting up for any other reason.[6]

All this religious instruction, perserveringly conducted week in and week out by cohorts of clergy in church schools up and down the land, had its amusing moments but, more seriously, it was disappointing to find its results to be meagre or at least not so splendid as it had been hoped. The country incumbent especially had a firm grip on the children of his parish through the school, would see that every child attended and, should it be absent, would call round to find why this was so. At Finmere in Oxfordshire all the children were required to attend day as well as Sunday school, except where special leave of absence was given; a soup dinner of half an ox-head at a time was provided twice a week and each child received a complete set of clothes. Yet the system was defective somewhere for though many had a certain amount of religious knowledge, they disappointed so often in their religious practice. On Sundays the children went to church, where they might be out of sight and sit, sleep, sprawl or whisper incessantly before rushing out of church 'like a pack of impatient dogs shod with iron'. When older, they would absent themselves from church altogether and jeer at the congregation, while the young men would lapse into idleness and drunkenness and the young women into immodesty, this being the rule in agricultural parishes.[7] Nevertheless, it was better to have schools than not to have them. They might bring disappointments, but through a school a vicar could touch the whole of his parish and it was his right hand.

The children of dissenters were cuckoos in the nest of some Anglican schools, since in the countryside there were usually no other schools than those established by the Church of England and dissenting children must attend them if they were to go to school at all. Until about 1840 there was much variety in the treatment that they received, for while some were subjected to the whole Anglican regime, others were excused classes that were concerned with catechism. Tractarianism, however, hardened attitudes against an easy-going approach to the dissenters and the National Society refused to allow schools to insert a conscience clause in their Trust Deeds so that in their schools the whole of the Anglican belief was taught to all the children. In 1860 the Privy Council started to demand a conscience clause in some schools, beginning in

Wales where Anglicanism was weakest; but if the State made a grant on condition that there was a conscience clause, the National Society refused to make a grant, which put the clergy in a dilemma. The Education Act of 1870 kept denominational schools, though it insisted on the conscience clause, maintaining that such schools were harmless to the children of other denominations since the secular teaching was secular and, if the school were Anglican, it was possible to avoid the vicar, the catechism and the Prayer Book. But, in fact, few children were withdrawn from Anglican instruction in Anglican schools, for, in 1887, when there were more than two million children on the registers of these schools, only two thousand two hundred were withdrawn from all religious instruction and only five thousand six hundred and ninety more when the catechism was taught, so that there was no great animus against the Anglican clergy and their teaching.

The Act of 1870 gave birth to a new kind of school, which grew steadily into a giant. Board schools were to be set up in places where there were no other schools or an inadequate number of schools, which was chiefly in the towns, and there were to be locally elected school boards, which had the power to levy rates, build schools, appoint teachers and, if they thought fit, to insist on all children attending, provided that they were not being educated in any other way. Also, the Cowper-Temple clause laid down that religious instruction in these schools should exclude any catechism or religious formulary distinctive of any particular denomination, so the clergy were excluded and their authority lessened, since it followed that in these schools religious instruction was in the hands of teachers who could teach the Bible in any way they pleased, provided that it was not the way taught by any particular denomination. The Act established, therefore, 'a new sacerdotal class', as Disraeli called it. For Bishop Stubbs it meant that the limitation of definite teaching was in the hands of those who believed the least. In the majority of board schools in Lincolnshire the Bible was taught without note or comment and in Nottinghamshire the Apostles' Creed was not taught at all, which filled Bishop Christopher Wordsworth with foreboding and led him to ask, 'How can men be made good citizens unless they are taught that all authority is from God?' And 'How can the rights of Property be maintained against the assaults of Socialism and Communism?'[8]

But board schools had come to stay and the clergy on the whole took up a wary and guarded attitude towards them, for Bishop Talbot at Rochester found that his clergy were for the most part respectful and sometimes friendly in their dealings with them. Enthusiastic incumbents might be elected to school boards, like Brooke Lambert, who startled his parishioners at Tamworth by walking down the street on a Sunday afternoon in a black velvet jacket, smoking a cigar, and who welcomed the school board there, though his views on the amount to be expended on school buildings, which would have fallen on the rates, were regarded as extravagant so that he refused to stand for the board again in 1877.

The clergy with Anglican schools were affected more seriously by these rival establishments in another way, for after 1870 there existed the possibility that Church of England schools which could not obtain sufficient support for their activities from subscriptions and elsewhere, might have to be handed over to the management of a school board. Richard Jefferies maintained that there was no demand from other denominations for this to happen, since they were neutralised by their own divisions and content to see the landowner and his party pay for Anglican schools; otherwise, if a school board took charge, the annual expenses of education would fall on the rates. But the burden of raising money for church schools was heavy and sometimes, in these situations, the money could not be found. Bishop Thorold of Winchester, who lived at Farnham Castle and looked down like any feudal lord upon the town of Farnham, was distressed to find that while he had been away at Torquay recovering from asthma, the inhabitants of Farnham had decided that they could not raise the seven to eight thousand pounds required for their church schools and had handed them over to a school board for management.

The day schools occupied six days of the week, though not

Saturday afternoon, and the Sunday schools might fill the seventh. In origin Sunday schools were not primarily concerned with religion, but with the task of teaching children who were at work on every other day but Sunday. At Bolton, Lancashire, in the 1770s the school met only on Sundays, from nine to ten fifteen before the morning service and from one forty-five to two forty-five before evening prayer, and attracted fourteen hundred pupils between the ages of ten and twenty, who learnt reading and writing from a hundred teachers. Robert Raikes, an evangelical layman at Gloucester, began a Sunday school in 1780, which is usually regarded as the beginning of the movement, and in his will directed that the children should follow his remains to the grave and each be given a shilling and a plum cake. It was a movement to keep the children off the streets and out of mischief, a movement to prevent crime and disorder, which was the primary purpose of the author of a *Plan for the Establishment and Regulation of Sunday Schools*, published in 1805, and the school hours could be sometimes as long as those in a day school, though protests were raised against this. If the Sunday school met before morning service, it meant that the two together occupied not less than three hours; and if another hour was demanded in the afternoon, the Lord's day became a day of mental toil rather than one of rest or happiness. Samuel Wilberforce wanted the children to be happy and advised Sunday school teachers in 1867 not to wake them if they fell asleep and to let them kick their legs about when sitting on a bench, if they wished to do so.[9]

Sunday schools were regarded with some suspicion at first in the Church of England, for the Prayer Book directed the clergy to catechise the children on Sundays in church during the course of evening prayer, and not to teach them on that day in the school; but they became so firmly established that in 1888 only forty-eight among the six hundred and eighty parishes in the diocese of Norwich did not have one. Many were inefficient, with untrained teachers and a dearth of male ones, but not all were in that category, for three lord chancellors in succession taught in Sunday schools and at Haworth the three Brontë sisters taught in theirs. In the north especially they were large, the Sunday school at Stockport in Cheshire claiming to be the largest in England with about five thousand members at the end of the nineteenth century, and often they ran themselves, keeping out the vicar who, if he were wise, welcomed this lay initiative. When the Sunday school anniversary came round, vast numbers would parade the streets, drumming up enormous enthusiasm, singing hymns, running races and having tea; and it was for one such occasion that Baring-Gould wrote the words of 'Onward, Christian Soldiers', which his Sunday school children were to sing at Horbury Brig when they marched up the hill to join the children of the parish church, though the well-known tune by Arthur Sullivan came later.

Vicars who valued education might initiate other activities in their parishes to help teach their people. Night schools had a fair following, catering for those who had left school while young, or who had never been to school, and bringing young people into direct and frequent contact with the clergy. Or the clergy might set up a course of lectures on such subjects as astronomy, geology and chemistry. Penny Readings, in which the parishioners entertained each other, were popular and Kilvert spent a day in 1871 preparing for one at which one hundred and sixty-seven were present; he recited from the 'Deserted Village', but not well, he thought, and afterwards there were red herrings for supper at the vicarage. Incumbents held Bible classes for adults and might provide reading-rooms. At Eversley there was a reading-room for men, with books, bagatelle and games, in which Kingsley sanctioned the provision of a good cask of beer, each glass of which was to be paid for on the spot in the hope that the men would not visit the public houses on the way home; but the seven public houses for the eight hundred people proved to be too influential and the reading-room was eventually shut up. Leeds had a reading-room open every night from seven to nine p.m., with classes for history, arithmetic, drawing and divinity, and lectures given in such subjects as experimental philosophy and physiology; and had over six hundred members. At King's Somborne a lending library was freely used by the villagers and gave them new interests; neighbours gathered by night in cottages to hear a book read to them and books even triumphed over beer, for the public house lost some of its attraction; old men learnt happily from their encyclopaedic grandchildren and children were so engrossed in their books that the clock ticked on unheeded.[10]

The upper classes had governesses for their younger children and were in the habit of sending their older boys away to school, so that the parish clergy were not often concerned with the education of these children; and the increasing popularity of the public schools in the nineteenth century meant that more of the children of the middle classes also were educated outside the parishes in which their parents lived. But there were still numerous private day and boarding schools, especially in the towns, and the clergy were urged to offer to go into them, perhaps weekly for an hour or more, and not to act as though they only had the care of the children of the poor.

In a few places the parochial clergy were able to interest themselves in more specialised forms of education, like the training of teachers or governesses. Henry Venn Elliott, who had charge of a proprietary chapel in Brighton, founded St. Mary's Hall to take an hundred girls for training as governesses for the children of the upper and middle classes, realising that the prospects of the daughters of some clerical families would not allow them to hope for better positions than these. He instanced a clergyman in a northern township, who was a gentleman and his wife a lady, with a pleasant house, paddock and pony and a parish well cared for, the schools well built and filled. But the income of the living was only ninety-two pounds a year and the house, which was not a parsonage, was rented for twenty-eight per annum, while the pony earned his food by drawing coals. St. Mary's Hall flourished, meeting the needs of the daughters of such families, though it had its difficulties and Elliott had one folder labelled 'Thorns and Prickles' containing correspondence with incompetent governesses, unreasonable parents, curious visitors and defaulting subscribers.[11]

Many and various, then, were the forms of education in which the clergy could dabble. They would find the work hard and it was essentially one of vexation and weariness, J. R. Woodford, then vicar of Leeds, told those being ordained at Banbury in 1861.[12] Some thought that too much stress was laid on religious education and it was pointed out that though a small proportion of the Christian world had been able to read, yet the assumption was growing that there could be little religion in those unable to read the Bible. But if the effect of religous education on children was doubtful, it was generally agreed that it was beneficial to the clergy who taught them, since it made vicars train themselves to simplify what they knew in order to give that knowledge to the children, and this might spill over into other channels. Sermons might become clearer and clerical feet planted more firmly on the earth.

NOTES

1   R. M. Grier, *John Allen*, p. 111.
2   H. J. Burgess, *Enterprise in Education*, pp. 32, 38.
3   John Sandford, *Parochialia*, pp. 80, 85–6.
4   R. W. Evans, *The Bishopric of Souls*, p. 155.
5   F. Smith, *History of English Elementary Education*, p. 162.
6   E. B. Ellman, *Recollections of a Sussex Parson*, pp. 239, 272.
7   J. W. Burgon, *A Treatise on the Pastoral Office*, pp. 244–7.
8   Christopher Wordsworth, *Ten Addresses*, pp. 118–20.
9   Ashwell and Wilberforce, *Samuel Wilberforce*, Vol. III, p. 228.
10 F. Smith, *op. cit.*, p. 201.
11 Josiah Bateman, *Henry Venn Elliott*, pp. 149, 155.
12 James Russell Woodford, *Ordination Sermons*, p. 38.

CHAPTER 9

The Wider Church

THE PARISH CLERGY were not much bothered with bishops at the beginning of the nineteenth century, though they belonged to an episcopal church, for an energetic bishop was a rarity at the time. If active, he might involve himself in the activities of the House of Lords or write books or visit the gentry and nobility of his diocese; and when he grew old he did not retire but gently declined in his palace while the world went by. The country parishes, anyway, were difficult to visit before the coming of the railways and so bishops rarely came to them. When Kilvert visited the vicar of Glascwm in Radnorshire he asked what happened if the vicar were ill. 'I give them a holiday,' was the reply. 'I am bishop here,' he said, and then, fetching the church key, added, 'Come and see the Cathedral.'

But bishops were necessary, needed, among other things, for confirmation, which according to the rules of the Church of England, they alone could administer. The Prayer Book was specific in its directions that as soon as children came to a competent age and could say in their mother tongue the Creed, the Lord's Prayer and the Ten Commandments, and answer the questions in the catechism, they should be brought to the bishop to be confirmed by him; and that no one should receive the communion until they had been confirmed or were desirous to be so. Bishops, therefore, held confirmations from time to time though, in the early years of the century, infrequently and mainly in the towns, so that the number of candidates being presented was often huge. The Master of Jesus College, Cambridge, remembered being confirmed in those years at Grantham, along with seven or eight thousand others in a scene of indescribable confusion, with oranges being sold in the church and the public houses ready to receive the congregation when it came out. William Cecil, rector of Long Stanton, near Cambridge, took his candidates to a confirmation at St. Michael's Cambridge in 1830. They set out at eight a.m. and reached the church at ten thirty where they sat till three p.m. without any prospect of getting the children confirmed, in a scene of turmoil, noise, talking, laughing, crying out and struggling, with young men and women indecently crowded together and some sitting on the pew backs or standing on the pews. The service began at eleven fifteen with the litany and then the bishop began to confirm in the chancel; after two or three hours many of the females began to faint, so the bishop ordered none but the girls to be admitted. There followed the bishop's charge and then silence, from which William Cecil deduced that the bishop had retired, but one boy, climbing over some high pews, reached the chancel doors and, squeezing his body through one of the open panels in the upper part of the door, got into the chancel. This display of initiative was imitated by half-a-dozen other boys, but Cecil himself and his boy candidates did not get into the chancel until about three o'clock when he had his gown rent and his coat torn. In the chancel there was chaos and the boys were confirmed, not in any order but coming up as they would. They left the church at four p.m. though one of his boys was detained a further hour by an officious doorkeeper to hear the bishop's charge read for a third time.[1]

Not all confirmations in those years were so chaotic, how-ever. A few years before the scuffling at St. Michael's Cam-bridge, nine hundred and eighty-four candidates had been presented at Bedale in Yorkshire in a service which had been excellently arranged, at which the bishop gave a most appro-priate address and for which the rector deserved very great praise, particularly for having put carpet down in the church to deaden the noise of the country people's hobnails against the flagstones.

The numbers coming to confirmation increased during the century, as vicars became more zealous and bishops more diligent, more numerous and, thanks to the railways, more mobile. Bishop Harold Browne confirmed in the Channel Islands within a year of his arrival in the diocese of Winchester in 1873, though it entailed a sea voyage and he hated the sea. Archbishop Vernon Harcourt of York, who died in 1847, would appear in York Minster, ascend to the pulpit and, extending his hands over the congregation, would pronounce the words of confirmation once; but William Thomson, who went to York as archbishop in 1862, was prepared to hold a confirmation in any village which had ten candidates to offer, and under his regime the cakes and sherry supplied for consumption in the vestry when the service was over, vanished. Then, too, there were more bishops for the work. In 1870 two suffragan bishops were appointed, one to assist the Archbishop of Canterbury, the other the Bishop of Lincoln; and dioceses were divided, bringing yet more bishops upon the scene. The diocese of Exeter, which covered Devon and Cornwall, gave up Cornwall to a new bishopric of Truro by Act of Parliament in 1876 and Edward White Benson went to be its first bishop and to live in a palace that was a stately Queen Anne house possessing large gardens on a hill overlooking Truro and the tidal estuary. More bishops meant more confirmations and consequently, though the total number of those being confirmed continued to grow, confirmations became more manageable, because fewer candidates need be presented at each service so that the unseemly crush of earlier years was done away.

Even so, the number of candidates presented at one service could still be large, and this, together with the propensity of bishops to speak at length and to give two addresses, might make the service a long one, though in the Prayer Book it could hardly be more brief. At Newington, London, there was a confirmation in 1880 with nearly six hundred candidates, which lasted three and three-quarter hours; when Bishop Thorold first entered the church he created a certain dramatic effect in the use of his cap, gloves and handkerchief which pained his friends. Bishop Otter of Chichester would speak to the children at a confirmation for a quarter of an hour before confirming them, and for some twenty minutes after doing so. He would tell them that they were doomed to eternal happiness or misery after the short period of the trial of life was passed, that they should be innocent and patient, read the Scriptures frequently and mind the company that they kept.[2]

Some of the parish clergy did not accept the new earnestness with which confirmation was administered, being content with the older ways, to the chagrin of their bishops. Samuel Wilberforce, who did much to make confirmation more edifying, once at a confirmation asked all the clergy to kneel down and join in intercession. But one stood up and talked to the clergyman next to him, which brought reproving but unheeded glances from the bishop, who eventually sent his apparitor to ask the miscreant to come and speak to him. He did, and the bishop told him that he would beg him to stay near him so that he would not be tempted to talk. 'Poor man!' wrote Wilberforce afterwards, 'He is quite, I fear, hardened in ungodliness and utter neglect of his parish: and a very clever, energetic man, too.'[3] In Sussex the vicar of Alfriston disapproved of confirmation altogether and the bishop, having decided to hold the service there, found on his arrival that the vicar was away. The clerk took Bishop Gilbert into the vestry, where a bottle of port wine and sandwiches had been provided, together with a roaring fire though it was a very hot summer's day.

There was no upper age limit on confirmation; at one service held near Halifax an old woman who was confirmed said after to a clergyman's wife, 'A turned sick three times, but a banged through!' Nor did the Prayer Book specify any lower age limit, though it laid down certain conditions to be fulfilled before candidates were presented. Bishop Blomfield thought that the age should be sixteen; John Gott, who was Dean of Worcester and had been vicar of Leeds, believed that there could be no hard and fast age of fifteen, but that anyone between thirteen and eighteen might be suitable, according to circumstances. Bishop Thorold told his clergy in 1881 that he would not confirm children that were under twelve, but nearly fifty years before that, Archbishop Whately had said to the clergy of Dublin that he thought some children under eleven could be well prepared for confirmation. There was, therefore, no universally acknowledged rule on the matter and bishops were themselves at variance on this question.

The clergy were advised to prepare a list privately of those who should be confirmed, then ask for candidates, then compare the list of those who offered with those on his own list, and then go out and see those who had not come forward. He must go out to the loutish crew who lounge in the high-way or infest the public house.[4] It was not usually regarded as necessary to have a lengthy period of preparation for confirmation, since the children would be well grounded in Prayer Book, catechism and Bible in their days at school, and bishops anyway did not always give much notice of the dates and places where they were going to confirm. Ashton Oxenden thought it would be good if bishops gave longer notice, for otherwise the preparation was limited to six or seven weeks. Before the riotous confirmation at St. Michael's, Cambridge, already described, the clergy had not more than ten days in which to prepare their candidates, so the rector of Long Stanton gathered his children for one or two evenings in the chancel and spoke to them from a chair; but on the other hand, John Keble prepared Charlotte Yonge for confirmation in 1838 and saw her twice a week from August to October. Six weeks, however, was about the normal time for preparation, after which the vicar would give his candidates tickets to be presented at the church where the confirmation was to be held so that all could be done there decently and in order; and if it were a country confirmation at another village, it was good to walk there in silence, or at least without mirth and clamour. At all costs candidates must be kept from the public house.

As the anglo-catholic movement made headway, and a

more elaborate ceremonial was introduced into some churches, the custom of dressing girls in white for confirmation was adopted, against the advice of some bishops who preferred that they should wear their ordinary Sunday clothes. Veils, too, began to be worn, and since elaborate finery was singularly out of place on such an occasion, it was recommended that a church should have a uniform set of them, to be worn by rich and poor alike. But the poor preparing for confirmation were concerned with the more basic need of acquiring fundamental garments, like the girl in Flora Thompson's confirmation class who, when asked by the rector's daughter if she was thoroughly prepared, piped up, 'Yes, miss, me mother says have you got a pair of your old boots you could give me, for I haven't got any fit to go in.' She got her boots.

The confirmed were not usually expected to rush to communion and, indeed, it would have been impossible to do so in parishes where the communion was only celebrated quarterly. But there was also a reluctance on the part of the newly-confirmed in some parts to go to communion, apparently because there was a dread of appearing conspicuous, and to overcome this problem it was suggested that communion might be at an early hour, when few could see them and they might thus surreptitiously receive the sacrament.

In the Middle Ages, when bishops went round the country confirming, they took the opportunity of inspecting their parishes and their clergy at the same time, and the Anglican Canons of the seventeenth century assumed that these two episcopal activities would go together, being undertaken every third year. It was hard work, for the bishops were not only bumped from place to place over bad roads, but faced enormous crowds at the confirmations, so that Bishop Gibson of Lincoln in the eighteenth century separated the confirmations from the visitations in his vast diocese, finding this more convenient and, though taking longer, less taxing on his strength. It was a policy adopted on a larger scale in the nineteenth century, when travelling became easier and bishops more inquisitive about the state of the parishes and the activities of the clergy, who found themselves every three years under scrutiny from above.

Visitations were preceded by the sending out of a set of questions to the parishes, asking details of the churches, the incumbents and other clergy, the services, and parochial activities generally; and when these were returned and the bishop had digested them, he would summon his clergy and churchwardens to meet him and deliver a charge. Victorian visitations were long, for there might be an hour's sermon and a charge lasting two hours, before the congregation left the church for a well-earned dinner. Campbell Tait delivered his first charge as Bishop of London, which included an attack on systematic confession, in St. Paul's Cathedral on a November afternoon in 1858 and spoke for nearly five hours. His biographers claimed that his steady, sonorous voice reached every ear from beginning to end, yet a month later when St. Paul's began Sunday evening services Tait boomed into the dome for nearly an hour and even those in the front barely distinguished a word, so perhaps the biographers were over-optimistic. 'Eyewitnesses,' they wrote, 'have often described how the short November day sank into twilight, then into darkness, and still, in clear, quiet, earnest tones he went on, the only object visible in the great building (for the dome was then unlighted), turning his pages by the light of two small lamps upon the temporary desk from which he spoke.' But did some of his hearers creep away in the darkness to meet the needs of nature? After the visitation was over, Tait was so exhausted that he had to go to Brighton to recuperate.[5]

The clergy had to sit quiescent while the charge was being read, keeping their thoughts to themselves, though if there were a dinner after, their tongues were loosened and sometimes uproar ensued. At the visitation at Lewes in 1850 there was a strong protestant sermon by Dr. Wellesley, Master of New Inn Hall, Oxford, and at the dinner that followed the bishop asked the archdeacon to propose the preacher's health, who, instead of praising the sermon, pointed out its defects. Someone rose to propose that the sermon be printed, and the large majority of those present shouted 'Print it! Print it!' The bishop said that for his part he would like to see the sermon in print but the clergy were not unanimous and the dinner broke up in some confusion.

In their charges the bishops dealt with the ecclesiastical problems of their day; confession and scepticism, sermons and education, dissenters and the Church of Rome, the poverty of the clergy and the state of their dioceses. To take an example, Archbishop Benson, at his third visitation of the diocese of Canterbury gave addresses at different centres, beginning at Canterbury Cathedral, where he spoke of parish councils, soon to be formed, and how vicars, though they might not be *ex officio* head of them, nevertheless had a place in them if they were wise, broad-minded and tactical. He wanted to know if parish rooms were securely vested in the church, for otherwise they might pass into the hands of parish councils. The next address, again at Canterbury, was devoted to non-sectarian education, and then, at Maidstone, he spoke on the need to encourage originality in children while teaching them, making the pleasant suggestion that 'it would be a most profitable pastime two or three times a week, if each class had its quiet reading time, lolling happily on the desks, over some sufficiently engrossing story, not to be questioned about afterwards'. This would arouse interest which might not be aroused in any other way. 'The little spirit must itself be charmed.' At Croydon he turned to movements in society, warning the clergy not to meddle in disputes which required technical knowledge, and then moved on to biblical criticism, which he thought did not need to be left to the scholars, for intelligent readers could look at the subject for themselves. He believed that the results of criticism would confirm the historicity of the Bible. And then, at Ashford, he asserted that the Church was conscious of steady progress in all directions and, because the Roman Catholic bishops had just refused to admit the validity of Anglican ordination, turned his guns against them, exclaiming, 'What a moment is this to be fingering the trinkets of Rome!'[6]

By the end of the century, visitations, in which the bishops gave their views and their dioceses listened reverently to what they had to say, were being displaced by diocesan synods, in which the clergy of the diocese met for discussions with their bishops, and diocesan conferences, in which the laity also joined. The bishop came down from his throne and became a chairman; and the tongues of the dumb, clerical and lay alike, began to speak.

Archdeacons as well as bishops held visitations. B. J. Armstrong attended one arranged by his archdeacon in 1853 and found it vexatious and wearisome. 'The sermon was inordinately long, the preacher indulging in a desultory attempt at poetry and eloquence which was wearying enough. His text was 'Ye are the light of the world', a description which, he emphatically said, after the clergy applied to the churchwardens. When one knows the amount of illumination possessed by farmers generally and Norfolk ones particularly the remark struck me as being ludicrous in the extreme. Fortunately the "charge" was not so long winded as the sermon.' Thirty years later he went to another archdeacon's visitation and found one rector, who was also a doctor of divinity, in full dress and a scarlet gown, while another was dressed in a morning coat. He lamented that neither of these men had a sense of the fitness of things.[7]

Though they also spoke of the larger affairs of the Church in their charges, archdeacons tended to dwell more than bishops did on more mundane matters such as church drains and windows. J. C. Hare told the clergy of his archdeaconry of Lewes in 1842 that religious newspapers were a sort of vermin springing up in the stagnant mud of the press, reported that since 1834 there had been an increase of above twenty per cent in the number of illegitimate children baptised, which was not entirely due to the working of the Poor Law but perhaps was to some extent so, and advised his clergy to scrape the whitewash from the pillars, arches and stonework of their churches. He assured them that they would be surprised at the change. When Bishop Blomfield had a stroke in 1855, the archdeacons of London and Middlesex ran the diocese and on being told that their charges for that year were on preaching and intramural burials, observed,

'Ah! I see, composition and decomposition.'

Increasing activity by bishops and archdeacons, which was directed sometimes at the parochial clergy even when there was not a visitation, might meet with resistance, sometimes because the parish clergy did not wish to be disturbed from their torpor but sometimes because they believed bishops and archdeacons were becoming officious and meddlesome. W. F. Hook, who was certainly not indolent, summed up his attitude to bishops in 1839. There were, first, those who might be termed spiritual peers, who associated with the other clergy as the lord-lieutenant of a county associated with the inferior magistrates, and these were generally the best, though not apparently the most active, since they did not needlessly interfere with parish priests, but were always ready to assist them. Other bishops, however, were like schoolmasters; and others, again, considered the whole diocese to be one parish and every parish priest the bishop's curate. They were the most busy prelates, but they had forgotten the authority, rights and privileges of priests who possessed authority, rights and privileges scarcely inferior to their own. Kingsley twenty years later would have heartily endorsed those sentiments, though he would have put archdeacons in the place of bishops, for he found his own archdeacon to be too inquisitive for his own liking. In 1858 the archdeacon had asked for information on the church and its fabric, and the schools, which were subjects within his province; but he asked also about pastoral visiting, which led Kingsley to write to Bishop Sumner protesting that such an enquiry could lead to 'an inquisitorial superintendence of parishes, fatal to that position as free rectors, which I hold to be one of the greatest safeguards and blessings of the Church of England'. But the archdeacon was not finished yet, for two years later he was writing again to ask the clergy for their views on *Essays and Reviews*, which had aired the disconcerting opinions of seven Anglican clergymen on the Bible, and this time Kingsley protested to the rural dean. He was prepared, he said, to express his opinion as one private gentleman to another, but the practical effect of this circular was inquisitorial and nothing else.[8]

A lower form of ecclesiastical life than that of bishop or archdeacon was that of a rural dean, who in a vague way was charged with the oversight of a small group of parishes and was usually himself the incumbent of one of the parishes in the group. With the increasing earnestness of the clergy and their tendency to live within their parishes, the possibility of a gathering of clergy meeting under the chairmanship of a rural dean became more feasible and was considered to be desirable, though the bishops had hesitations about the outcome of such gatherings. Bishop Otter wrote a letter to the rural deans of the diocese of Chichester in which he noted, among other things, that Anglican clergy met together very little, but that when they did meet they either shrank from each other or argued. Nevertheless, he asked that they should meet together in their deaneries at least once a quarter. The Archdeacon of Middlesex spent his charge of 1845 on this subject of ruri-decanal chapters. They had been instituted, he said, by the bishop, in response to the desire of the clergy for personal intercourse and the result seemed to have been good, for no one had been offended; but then the bishop had ruled that there should be no discussion of theological controversy or of the general policy of the Church. Subjects should be of a strictly practical kind and there was to be no printed publication of the proceedings in order that publicity might be avoided.[9]

Some of the clergy, like Baring-Gould, never attended these meetings, but many did and discussed matters of parochial concern. One such was held at Chippenham Town Hall in 1874 on the subject of 'how to wake a parish', which turned out to be a misprint for 'how to work a parish', and ranged over a wide variety of topics, from the need of the clergyman to confine himself to his own parish, to night school and Bible classes, taking in guilds and weekly communion on the way. One incumbent spoke out strongly and in bad taste against the dissenters and the rural dean himself unwisely introduced the subject of contagious diseases and the enforced surgical examination of suspected women.

The clergy did not meet together only when the bishop or

archdeacon or rural dean considered that they should do so, but gathered in groups less formally to reform the Church or to maintain its rights, to protest against this suggestion or to support that movement, or maybe merely to meet in order to enjoy each other's company in the convivial atmosphere of a clerical club. Occasionally such a meeting might be important as, in retrospect, the Hadleigh Conference was thought to be, to which Hugh James Rose, editor of the *British Magazine* but also rector of Hadleigh invited Hurrel Froude and William Palmer from Oxford that they might discuss the formation of a society to defend the liberties and principles of the Church. The meeting decided nothing, except that the suppression of ten Irish bishoprics by a Whig government forced them to proclaim that the Christian ministry possessed a divine authority independent of the State. Later the conference came to be regarded as a clerical conspiracy, but it was no such thing, though it contributed to the initial stages of the Oxford Movement. Nothing of great importance, however, came out of a meeting in 1874 when J. B. Armstrong dined at North Tuddenham in Norfolk with the clergy of the deanery who had voluntarily come together in a society for mutual improvement; the dinner was far too good, Armstrong thought, but then the rector who gave it was a rich man and had no children.

There remained always some incumbents who were square pegs in round holes, who found themselves in the wrong profession or the wrong parish and could not get out. A Mr. Williams had been presented to the rectory of Widecombe-in-the-Moor by the Dean and Chapter of Exeter. He was an able man but no parish priest, having been forced by his father to take orders so that he might occupy a family living; but his father died before he could be presented to it and he found himself at Widecombe. He hated the Moor, and had no interest in the place, the people or the church. 'I feel,' he said, 'like Noah in the Ark, surrounded by beasts, but unlike him, without a dove in it—only jackdaws, magpies and starlings—and,' after a pause, 'any number of geese.'

As far as vicars were concerned, dissenters were the black

sheep of the Church's flock, claiming to be Christian yet rejecting the Church of England and her ministers. Anglican clergymen were sure that a vicar had the duty to minister to every person in his parish, of whatever religious persuasion that they happened to be. Their attitude towards dissenters, however, varied greatly, ranging from open hostility to a frosty friendliness; and it varied, too, according to the type of dissent that was encountered. The curates at Haworth spoke fiercely against dissenters, much to the chagrin of the Brontë sisters; their much loved cook, Tabby, belonged to the Keighley Methodist Church. John Allen recognised the good work that the Primitive Methodists had done at Prees, where their encouragement of sobriety and thrift had brought about a reduction in the number of public houses in the parish from ten to two in the space of thirty years; and in Cornwall the vicar of Kenwyn enjoyed good relations with the Methodist minister at a hamlet in the parish, who consulted him when boys broke the windows of his little chapel. Bishop Light-foot, in his first charge to the diocese of Durham, urged his hearers to be friendly to the Salvationists who had done much good, he thought, and were filled with missionary zeal, though they were sensational. At Bath one day Francis Kilvert slipped into the catholic church and offered up a prayer for unity.

On the other hand, incumbents were often hostile to the sheep that were not of their fold. Charles Kingsley was prepared to describe the local Baptist pastors as 'muck enthroned on their respective dung hills, screeching on their scrannel pipes of ragged straw', and claimed that he never dared to leave his parish without thoroughly tarring his sheep to keep off the schismatic flies and mosquitoes who would be at them as soon as he was gone. Dissenters were a perplexing problem even to such an able and vigorous man as Samuel Wilberforce, who wrote to Hook who had recently become vicar of Leeds, describing dissent in his parish of Brighstone in the Isle of Wight and asking what should be done with the Ranters, a name commonly used in the nineteenth century for Primitive Methodists. He wrote:

Will you give me any practical suggestions as to managing the Ranter section of a parish? When I took possession of my present living, 8 years ago, I found in it a Wesleyan meeting, which had been some seven years rooted. The *regular afternoon* service of the village was with them, not above 12 persons being present at the prayers of the Church. By God's blessing on various plans I succeeded in regaining them so far to an outward conformity that at 2 years' end the meeting was closed and the Wesleyans left the parish. But a body of *Ranters* soon crept in from a neighbouring parish. They pretended affection to the Church, laid hold of the strongest Wesleyan villagers, got to prayer-meetings in cottages, by degrees weaned them from the Church, threw off the mask, and made a schism, and have now run up a meeting-house. They have about 30 or 35 regular members (out of a population of 700), but have large attendances from curiousity etc., etc. They touch none but the poorest and most ignorant. Their doctrine is Arminian—perfection, etc. Their arms, strong sensuous excitement, bodily perceptions of the presence of evil spirits, as well as of the Most Holy Spirit of God; their animosity to the Church extreme; their zeal for prose-lytising unbounded; their apparent sanctity considerable; their real self-righteousness fatal.[10]

Dissenters, then, were a thorn in the flesh of the Anglican clergy, some more so and some less, but must needs be tol-erated since they could not now be put in chains or burnt at the stake. If they could be converted to the ways of the Church of England, so much the better, but some caution had to be used in attempting this, especially with the very poor of the Church of Rome, who might be tempted to come over in order to gain financial benefits. The use of Anglican wealth in order to buy the allegiance of dissenters was sometimes tried, though it proved to be a two-edged weapon. An incumbent in the diocese of London had refused to grant parish allotments unless he had from the applicants for them a written promise that they would never again enter a meeting-house, which brought a stiff letter from Bishop Blomfield, who pointed out that the result was to take from nineteen or twenty families a great part of their means of subsistence in a wretchedly poor district. 'What you should aim at,' he wrote, 'is not to make men promise to come to Church, but to convince them of the duty of doing so.' The result of refusing allotments was to make dissent flourish.

A little reading might help to bring over the dissenter. Dr. Pusey's *Eirenicon*, which was strongly and Christianly anti-Roman according to Dr. Gott, was recommended to the parish priest of the town who became entangled with Roman Catholics. To convert the Wesleyans it was suggested that a reading of the principal parts of the first four volumes of Wesley's sermons together with his *Notes on the New Testament* might prove helpful. The Wesleyan stress on conversion should remind Anglicans of the importance of confirmation, which had often been neglected; Wesleyan ministers should be treated with perfect courtesy and respect, without abandoning Anglican principles, however. To combat Baptists, confirmation should again be stressed as the rightful alternative to adult baptism, and Unitarians should be met with full and clear teaching of the Three-in-One.

Rarely argue with dissenters, the clergy were advised, and though they might appear with dissenters on platforms where the subject was not of a religious nature, to appear with them when the subject was a religious one was considered inadvisable. To preach in a nonconformist chapel was almost unheard of, though the vicar of Greenwich announced in 1885 that he was proposing to preach in one in Paddington and was promptly summoned to meet his bishop, who remonstrated with him and pointed out that the seventy-first canon ordered the clergy not to preach in private houses. But a chapel was hardly a private house, so the vicar went and preached and no retribution, divine or episcopal, ensued.

More agreeable than the dissenters, because they were more remote and more romantic, were the Christians overseas who had been called into being through the missionary work of the Church, supervised by societies with their head-quarters at home in England. Evangelists sent out from Britain, with pith helmets and camp beds, battling through the jungle amidst hostile tribes, needed funds for their equipment and their work, and these were provided in substantial amounts by the parishes at home, which learnt through lectures and lantern slides of the heroic endeavours of these missionaries beyond the seas. Congregations were fascinated by descriptions of lands so barbarically different from their own and people came in large numbers to hear about them. At the end of October 1841, G. A. Selwyn, newly-elected Bishop of New Zealand, preached to a packed congregation in the parish church of Windsor on the claims of the heathen at the other side of the world. An Eton boy, in his white collar and short jacket, stood in the aisle, since every seat was taken, and after all was over, wrote home describing the scene. 'It was beautiful when he talked of his going out to found a church and then to die neglected and forgotten. All the people burst out crying, he was so very much beloved by his parishioners. He spoke of his perils and putting his trust in God, and then, when he had finished, I think I never heard anything like the sensation, a kind of feeling that, if it had not been on so sacred a spot, all would have exclaimed, "God bless him!" ' The boy's name was Patteson, destined one day to become Bishop of Melanesia and to die a martyr on the island of Nukapu in the Southern Seas.[11]

Not everyone was agreed that the sending of missionaries or their representatives round the parishes was a good thing. If such a deputation did come, some of the clergy regarded it as an opportunity to take a Sunday off and were warned against doing this, for it was better if they themselves preached on the missionary work of the Church overseas. Bishop Phillpotts went so far as to forbid representatives of home and foreign missions preaching in the pulpits of his diocese of Exeter, though he allowed them to hold meetings in other places than the church. 'Do not,' he said, 'encourage strangers to go through your churches, extolling, and sometimes exaggerating, with all the arts of rhetoric (as a stranger sent for the purpose is likely to do), the claims of the society which employs him. It is a great disturbance of the parochial system; it produces an unwholesome excitement; it turns God's house into a hall of declamation, too often pampering the diseased appetite for a tone of teaching which is neither milk nor strong meat, but a crude and mawkish substitute, by which no generous or manly growth of Christian charity was ever yet reared.'[12] He had support for his view, yet a returning missionary could bring to a parish an eye-witness account of the excitement of preaching the gospel to the heathen in a manner no resident vicar could emulate; and what better place could there be for the missionary to speak from than the pulpit?

To raise funds for the missionary societies a collection in church might be made. The Prayer Book authorised the taking up of a collection during the communion service 'for the Poor, and other devotions of the people', and since this collection came in the first part of the service it could still be made though the whole communion service was not to be used. There was some doubt as to what 'the other devotions of the people' might be, but learned legal opinion thought that these might legitimately include money given for the building of churches for the poor outside the parish and the work of propogating the gospel in foreign parts. So, at Dunchurch, there was a collection on the first Sunday of the month and on the festivals of the church and this was given on some occasions to missionary work. In a year running from 1843 to 1844, the parish gave twelve pounds to the Missions to Colonies in August 1843, and a similar amount to the Mission to Jews at the Christmas of that year; and then in February 1844, it gave £12. 2s. 8d. to the Missions to the Heathen, while the other collections in the year went to the poor, the parochial school, factory children and other causes. An alms-box in church for foreign missions could be useful, while bazaars, lectures on missionary work at which a collection might be taken, and recitals might be arranged to support the work of taking the gospel overseas. Charlotte Brontë describes in *Shirley* a Jew-basket, which was the name given to a good-sized family clothes-basket full of pincushions, needlebooks, cardracks, work-bags, articles of infant wear, etc., which had been made 'by the willing or reluctant hands of the Christian ladies of a parish, and sold perforce to the heathenish gentlemen thereof, at prices unblushingly exorbitant'. The proceeds went to support the missionary.

The nineteenth-century parish was not only conscious that, for the most part, the church was expanding at home but that overseas great multitudes were being brought into the fold. Here was a situation exhilarating and satisfactory, vividly illustrated in a hymn written by A. C. Ainger in 1894 predicting the continued growth of the church. One verse reads:

> From utmost east to utmost west where'er
>   Man's foot hath trod,
> By the mouth of many messengers goes forth
>   the voice of God.
> Give ear to me, ye continents, ye isles, give
>   ear to me,
> That the earth may be filled with the glory of
>   God as the waters cover the sea!

NOTES

1   *Confirmation*, by various writers, Vol. 1, pp. 213–15.
2   William Otter, *Pastoral Addresses*, pp. 116–22.
3   Ashwell and R. Wilberforce, *Samuel Wilberforce*, Vol. 1, p. 394.
4   J. W. Burgon, *A Treatise on the Pastoral Office*, p. 289.
5   R. T. Davidson and W. Benham, *Archibald Campbell Tait*, pp. 265–9.
6   E. W. Benson, *Fishers of Men*.
7   H. B. J. Armstrong, *Armstrong's Norfolk Diary*, pp. 37, 183.
8   Mary Kingsley, *Charles Kingsley*, Vol. 11, pp. 79, 80.
9   Archdeacon Sinclair, *Thirty-two Years of the Church of England*, pp. 33–6.
10   Ashwell and R. Wilberforce, *op. cit.*, Vol. 1, p. 127.

11 Jesse Page, *Bishop Patteson*, pp. 12–13.
12 G. C. B. Davies, *Henry Phillpotts*, p. 173.

CHAPTER 10

The Secular World

A POPULAR BOOK of advice to the parochial clergy, whose first edition appeared in 1842 and which reached a fifth edition thirty-five years later, advised them not to be magistrates. They would, however, be the mainspring of the police of their parishes even if they were not seen as such and this view of the clergy as hidden supporters of law and order—a kind of social cement—can be found everywhere in the nineteenth century. Hugh James Rose preaching before the University of Cambridge in 1826 thought that the utility of religion as a restraint on violence and cruelty was well recognised, and Lord Brougham told Parliament eight years later that the church-going habit helped at once to civilise the lower orders, to humanise the higher, and to bind them closer in a common society. Much later in the century the same attitude is expressed by such various figures as Taine, who saw the Church as the moral health department of the State, respect for Christianity being accepted by public opinion as a duty and even as an aspect of good behaviour; and Bishop Thorold who maintained in 1885 that a consequence of the disestablishment of the Church would be that the best and cheapest kind of police would be suddenly dismissed about their business. Another bishop, Woodford of Ely, reiterated the opinion that it was the Church that had given to national institutions a stability unparalleled in modern Europe.

The identification of the clergy with the forces of law and

order was most evident when they served as justices of the peace. There was good reason why they should do so, especially in rural areas, for they were usually assiduous in their work, like Blomfield who, being made a magistrate in 1813 when rector of Dunton in Buckinghamshire, would ride over to the petty sessions at Wing in yellow overalls to protect himself from the mud. They were also usually incorruptible, fully literate, with trained minds that could take in the law. The standard work on the duties of magistrates was written by Richard Burn, vicar of Orton in Westmorland. The accused, therefore, might stand a better chance of obtaining justice from clerical magistrates than from a posse of fox-hunting squires who lingered long over their port, and might prefer to appear before clerical gentlemen rather than landowners if they had been caught poaching. On the other hand, miscreants who offended against sobriety, morality and Sunday observance might find clerical justices more severe than their lay counterparts. The vicar of Kidlington, near Oxford, sentenced nine women in 1830 to between four and six weeks at the house of correction for 'night walking', and the rector of Broughton, Oxfordshire, made six convictions for drunkenness in 1860, with fines of ten shillings or six hours in the stocks. At Eynsham in 1847, the vicar charged a man with selling a pennyworth of walnuts on a Sunday.[1]

As the century went forward, public opinion hardened into the view that the clergy should not be magistrates, partly because more educated laymen became available to undertake this duty, partly because the clerical profession itself was becoming more demanding and time-consuming and partly because it came to be thought more and more that the two callings were incompatible. W. J. Butler at Wantage was never a magistrate, believing that 'preachee-preachee' and 'floggee-floggee' should not go together, and there was a sensational case in Oxfordshire in 1873, which aroused considerable criticism of clerical justices and hastened their decline. The union of agricultural workers set up by Joseph Arch was strong in the county and particularly strong at Ascot-under-Wychwood where the unionists went on strike.

Two lads of eighteen, therefore, were brought in to work on a farm and so aroused the wrath of sixteen Ascot women who molested them and endeavoured to make them leave their work. The women were charged before two clerical magistrates, the vicar of Shipton-under-Wychwood and the rector of Swerford, who sentenced them all to hard labour, some for ten days and some for seven. The sentences seemed severe and the Lord Chancellor was critical, could not understand why all of the women had been sent to prison and thought that the law would have been better served by taking a different and more lenient course. The women made a triumphal entry into their village, accompanied by a speech from Arch, and the number of clerical magistrates, which in that year was one thousand and forty-three, sank gradually to under forty by 1906.

It was all too easy to represent the clergy as the oppressors of the poor, if they were also magistrates, yet most vicars did not endeavour to grind the faces of their most indigent parishioners in the dust. By temperament the Anglican clergyman was usually conservative, thought that the stratification of the classes was a permanent feature of society, believed that the poor would always be with them and that, therefore, they should be content with their lot on earth, while hoping for better things in heaven. They did not concern themselves much with national movements like Chartism or the trade unions, but worked to ameliorate the worst effect of poverty in their own parishes, so much so that the Church was seen to be inextricably immersed in social work. Parish clergy, for instance, knew much about mangles, because they provided a modest livelihood for a woman who washed clothes. Someone proposed to set up another mangle in a short street in Brighton and H. V. Elliott, who was in charge of St. Mary's Church, was appealed to. He ruled against it. 'I cannot allow this to be done,' he said, 'this small street does not allow of more mangles than one, if people are to get their living.' The caretaker of a school in Bethnal Green met the mother of one of the children on a Sunday morning and exclaimed:

'Why, Mrs. Jones, you're out early.'
'Yes, sir. I'm going to church.'
'Going to church?'
'Yes, sir. I've lost my mangle.'[2]

To help the poor, incumbents might be able to call upon the generosity of past parishioners who had left money or land to be laid out in the provision of bread and coals and clothing for the needy, since in the majority of cases the clergy were involved in the administration of such charities, often being associated with the churchwardens in this task. The vicar of Yarnton, near Oxford, drew up a scheme for the administration of Alderman Fletcher's Charity in his parish in 1855, which was signed by himself, the churchwardens and other trustees. The scheme directed that only the poor of the parish should receive Christmas gifts, etc., and that on Christmas Day bread as well as meat should be distributed. On the alderman's burial day, January 4th, bread and cakes should be distributed in the aisle or porch of the church, the bread first and then the cakes, even if that day should be a Sunday, and the cakes should only be given to those children old enough to walk to church. A record should be kept of the amount of meat and bread distributed, its cost and the number of people who received them. The scheme restricted, perhaps unfairly, the charity to worshippers at the church, for it ended with the clause:

Seeing that the Alderman was a sincere and single-hearted Christian and an exact observer of the Sabbath Day, and seeing too that he expended considerable sums in new pewing Yarnton Church, and providing foot boards to keep the feet warm in Church, and seeing that he built a schoolroom, etc., we are of the opinion that in distributing the Bread, Meat and Cakes a distinction should be made between those who worship in that Parish Church that he fitted up, and those who seldom or never enter it. To conclude: it is recommended that in making out the lists of the year, all persons (males or females, boys or girls) whose conduct during the past year has been wicked, should be dropped out of the Charity lists.[3]

The feckless and the indolent saw in parochial charities a means of obtaining money, food or clothing for which they had not worked, and for this reason they were regarded as a mixed blessing by vicars and others who had to disburse their bequests. The Victorian clergy, therefore, looked more favourably on the many and various clubs, societies and associations which they established in their parishes and to which their poorer parishioners subscribed, even if only a mite, for in this way the poor learnt to practise thrift and fore-thought in the battle of life and were rewarded by benefits when they needed them. A benefit society, which provided a simple form of insurance, might be established, to which young and active working men could contribute, receiving in return a guaranteed weekly payment during sickness, an annuity in advanced age, a sum to bequeath in the event of his decease, and the means of binding a child to a trade or other-wise setting him out in life. But it was essential, if such a soc-iety were established, to have proper rules and that it should be based on sensible financial calculations, or else they would break up or the funds be misappropriated. Particulars of premiums and other details could be obtained from Charles Jellicoe Esq., 35, Old Jewry, London.

Provident funds, which worked on the same principle as the benefit societies but on a smaller scale, were concerned with the more mundane matters of providing fuel and food and rent and clothing. In a clothing club the parishioners might pay in a penny or sixpence a week, to which would be added a penny a week from the fund given by the benevolent persons of the parish. At the end of the year, tickets would be handed out to the club's members to be exchanged at the drapers for articles of clothing, though the members of the club might not have complete freedom of choice over their purchases, since the club's officers might check to see that the tickets were not used to buy light, useless finery.[4] At Horspath in Oxfordshire a 'Rent and Shoe Club' was founded in 1851. 'It is intended,' the vicar announced, 'to encourage those who are inclined to help themselves.' As a condition of membership one member of the family had to attend regular weekly prayers and no drunkard, Sabbath breaker or immoral person could belong. The vicar hoped that the club would help to reduce the excessive drinking in the village, and tempted his parishioners to join by promising to add two shillings to each subscription on St. Andrew's Day each year.

The enterprising incumbent might set up a dispensary or medical union for the benefit of the poor, the simplest form of which was for a doctor to agree to treat the parishioners in the dispensary or union for a fixed sum of money, which was raised from the parishioners themselves by weekly subscriptions; but this had disadvantages. In a year when there was much sickness, the doctor felt hard done by, was tempted to neglect his more unfavourable cases and to furnish medicines of an inferior quality, while the sick themselves felt embarrassed in accepting a great deal of treatment from the doctor which they well knew was not covered by their contributions to the fund. Also, some members of the union might default on their payments and the doctor then would be tardily paid, if paid at all. The energetic vicar of Dunchurch appears to have solved these problems by introducing a modification of this scheme by, first of all, obtaining from the local doctor the usual annual amount of receipts from his poorer patients for the previous five years and then guaranteeing to pay that amount himself in future to him. The poor then paid their subscriptions to the vicar, which were not sufficient to cover the doctor's charges, but the shortfall was made up by donations from wealthier members of the flock. The Medical Union at Dunchurch was restricted to members of the working class within the parish who were not receiving parochial relief, and those who earned twenty shillings or more a week and those whose earnings, together with those of their family under sixteen, amounted to thirty shillings or more, were excluded. Single persons paid two shillings and sixpence a year; a widow or widower with children paid four shillings and a married couple without children paid the same, while a married couple with children paid five shillings. Children over fourteen could not be included in their parents' subscriptions but must pay for themselves, and married women belonging to the Union were entitled to the necessary medical attention during childbirth provided that they paid eight shillings before their confinement. In the first year that the scheme was in operation, the poor paid £23. 13s. 6d. and the medical bills came to £40. 18s. 6d., the difference of £17. 5s. 0d. being supplied by the charitable contributions of the well-to-do. One year brought fifty-nine cases from members of the Union for treatment by the doctor. There were ten confinements, and afflictions ranged from a tumour on the head, pleurisy, fever, quinsy and a dropsical affection to a sprained knee and a cough.[5] In the towns these medical unions might be established on a large scale, like the one at Leeds set up by Dr. Hook in 1834 in which the subscriptions amounted to fifteen hundred pounds, allowing the committee to employ three surgeons at the rate of nearly three hundred pounds per annum for each of them. Less ambitious were clergymen like Sydney Smith who set up an apothecary's shop, which sold drugs and groceries, in his parish at Combe Florey, near Taunton.

In the country the vicar might help the poor by finding them allotments, perhaps on the glebe, but if he did this he was advised to make sure that certain conditions were first fulfilled. He must see to it that the local farmers had no objection to the scheme, and it was possible to achieve this if the amount of land made available for an allotment did not exceed what the holder of it, together with his family, could cultivate thoroughly with spade husbandry in their unoccupied and leisure hours. A rood was generally regarded as about the right amount of land if this requirement were to be met, and the land should be let at the same rate as it would be to a farmer, so that farmers could not complain of being treated less fairly than their workers. The creation of allotments, it was maintained, diminished drunkenness, made parishioners happier and more industrious, and helped them to climb several rungs of the social ladder if they showed prowess at cultivation. On light evenings, Flora Thompson recalled, the men, after a hard day's work in the fields and their tea-cum-supper in their cottages, would work strenuously in their gardens and allotments, while on moonlit nights in the spring the solitary fork of someone who had not been able to tear himself away from his land would be heard, and the man singing. The cottage gardens were kept for green vegetables and the pig; the allotments were usually divided into two and used, the one half for potatoes, the other for wheat or barley. If the land were glebe land, then the incumbent could insist that the tenant and his family attend divine service on Sundays and that they should on no account work on the land on that day. If the tenant were convicted of poaching, thieving, drunkenness, or any offence against the laws of the country, he must give up his lot at the Michaelmas ensuing. What spectacle so delightful, asked the Rev. John Sandford, 'as that of a healthy, industrious, contented, and religious peasantry—men civilised and attached by the influence of kindness—whom you found rude, lawless and estranged, because neglected—but whom the sympathy of the superior has reformed and won; and who, instead of being a ready prey to the incendiary and the democrat, are the cheap and loyal defence of property and law?'

Pigs were an important part of the domestic economy for many of the poor, who kept one each year, fattening it and then killing it. It gave bacon for the winter, ham, hog's pudding, chitterlings, and so a full larder and a varied one for a while. But if the pig died young, before its time, the tragedy was great and the vicar might come to the rescue of the pigless family by giving half-a-crown to soften the catastrophe.

Other means might be used by vicars to alleviate the miseries of the poor. They might campaign for better housing, urging landlords to improve their accommodation, or, like Canon Barnett at St. Jude's, Whitechapel, they might themselves become involved in the purchasing of sites and the rebuilding of houses with some regard to beauty. They might interest themselves in drains. 'Sanitary improvements come very naturally within a clergyman's province,' Archdeacon Fearon told the clergy of Leicester in a charge of 1865. They might hold a dinner once a year for old men or old women or arrange an annual excursion for children and their parents. From St. George's Mission in the parish of St. George's-in-the-East, London, five or six hundred parents and their children would go each year on an outing, by chartered steamer to Erith or by special train to Hampton Court, Box Hill or Chislehurst. The vicar's wife might provide soup in the parsonage kitchen for any who came to get it, and a layette for the parish babies which was passed from one to another as they arrived. All this was admirable and much good work was done, especially in the countryside where there were more clergymen and fewer people than in the towns; but there were drawbacks. The clergy, for their part, found that their charitable endeavours did not increase the religious commitment of the poor. The bulk of the agricultural labouring population, the strong, sturdy men, the carters and shepherds, stood aloof, Richard Jefferies observed, and cleaned their boots on Sundays when the church bells were ringing before walking down to their allotments. They had no quarrel with the church, but there was, as it were, a blank space between them. The problems of the poor, on the other hand, were too great to be solved, in the end, by the parochial clergy, who naturally thought in parochial terms, for it was the nation itself that alone could effectively tackle the enormous problem of nineteenth-century poverty.

Keble and his friends worked hard for the poor in their parishes but did not identify themselves with national movements for working-class improvement. A few parochial clergymen, however, did take an interest in them, like George Bull, one-time sailor and later famous for his support of the Factory Acts, who was ordained, became vicar of St. James's, Bradford, and wrote in 1839 *The Oppressors of the Poor and the Poor their own Oppressors* in which he denounced the oppressors in the fierce language of the Old Testament prophets. Charles Kingsley preached a Whitsun sermon at Eversley in which he equated the Kingdom of God with the socialist millennium and in response the two oboists and the horn player who comprised the church band struck up 'The Good Time Coming' and then invited him to a dinner. He played a significant part in the Chartist movement and in *Alton Locke*, founded on the life of the Chartist, tailor and poet, Thomas Cooper, pleaded the cause of the poor in language of rare power as he described their misery. 'What a room!' he wrote, 'a low lean-to with wooden walls, without a single article of furniture; through the broad chinks of the floor shone up, as it were, ugly glaring eyes . . . the reflections of the rushlight in the sewer below. The stench was frightful—the air heavy with pestilence. The first breath I drew made my heart shrink, and my stomach turn. But I forgot everything in the object which lay before me, as Downes tore a half-finished coat off three corpses laid side by side on the bare floor.' But better known than *Alton Locke* is Kingsley's attack on the exploitation of boy chimney-sweeps in *The Water Babies*.

The parochial clergy might wish to stand clear of Chartism and the like, but they could not avoid the trade unions, agricultural and otherwise, when they appeared in their parishes, nor the unemployed, when they banded together, demanded work and came to church in a body. In the countryside the clergy might find themselves impaled on the horns of a dilemma, for, on the one hand, they might think the demands of the labourers to be just, and, on the other, the need to keep the roof on the church and the teacher in the school might only be possible through the subscriptions of the squire and the farmers, so that there is little wonder that they reacted variously when faced with the challenge of the organised poor. The vicar of Leintwardine in Herefordshire helped to form a union which spoke firmly yet respectfully to the landlords, claimed a membership of thirty thousand, and had a dissenter as secretary and twenty clergymen as vice-presidents. But there were many at the other extreme and few would doubt, one socialist clergyman said, that the Church of England greatly needed the help of divine grace to preserve it from an undue reverence for station and property. The identification of the clergy with the rich hastened the decline of church-going among the working classes. Early in the 1890s a village parson in Devonshire on his way to church met a group of loafers and invited them to go with him. But they replied, 'No, and you wouldn't go unless you were paid for it.'⁶ Yet at about that time Flora Thompson recalled a new vicar at Candleford Green as a young man in his early thirties, who would run out to post a letter or buy a cucumber in his shirt-sleeves, help an old woman by carrying her sticks, and acknowledge that he was himself poor. A few of the parishioners sighed for the old regime, but the majority of them rejoiced in the new, democratic atmosphere of parochial life. The clergy varied greatly in their attitude towards the poor.

For nearly the whole of the nineteenth century the incumbent found himself inevitably and inextricably entangled in civic affairs since he was *ex officio* chairman of the vestry and the vestry concerned itself not only with church affairs but with secular matters also. The vestry of the parish of Walmer on the coast of Kent appointed two parish beadles in 1833 to conduct vagrants out of the parish and to detect 'depredators'; it paid them each nine shillings a week and equipped them with uniforms of a blue coat with red collar, staff and hat. In 1846 it considered the rival attractions of three possible railway lines through the parish, proposed respectively by the Dover and Deal Railway Company, the Cinque Ports, Thanet and Coast Junction Company and the North Kent Railway Company, and thought poorly of the first two suggestions since their routes would tend to annoy and endanger passengers, 'besides incessantly disturbing the quiet of this fashionable place of resort'. In the same year it appointed a paid constable at eighteen shillings a week and commanded him to report to the vicar every Monday morning between nine and ten; but the man, though formerly of the metropolitan police, proved unsatisfactory, for seven years later a committee had to be formed for the purpose of inducing him to attend to his duties in a more efficient manner. The vestry organised a cricket match on the Goodwin Sands, considered the supply of gas in the parish, made arrangements for the disposal of sewage, and congratulated itself in 1887 that whereas the death rate in neighbouring Deal was 14.8 per thousand, in Walmer it was 11 per thousand. Plans to annexe the parish to Deal were fought off with great vigour in 1862 when the vestry adjourned to the George and Dragon where it passed unanimously a resolution against the scheme. But it considered also church matters; pondered the provision of additional burial grounds, received thankfully the gift of an organ for the church from Mrs. Twopenny and regretted that the organist could not be paid out of the church rate.

With so many matters to consider, there was inevitably conflict at times within the vestry and that not always over ecclesiastical affairs. Ratepayers sought to keep down the rates, factions might form and uproar might follow, so that some incumbents, who were by nature or inclination or both unsuited for the chairmanship of such a body, shrank from that office, though Samuel Wilberforce urged his clergy in the diocese of Oxford to preside habitually in order to allay irritations and strifes.

But, more and more, other authorities such as the county council were given power in the parishes by Act of Parliament and the vestries themselves, it was widely acknowledged, needed reform, since the plural system of voting that they used meant that those with more property had more votes then those with less. In 1894, therefore, an Act set up parish councils, its members elected by ballot, and abolished plural voting. The vicar was no longer to be automatically the chairman, and might not even be a member unless he had been elected, though in most places his influence was strong and he continued to play an important part in the proceedings. At Welney in the fens, the parish council elected the master of the church school as its chairman who, with the support of the council, called the rector, who had been the former chairman, to order. The next day the rector dismissed the master from the school and from the harmonium, though the dismissal was afterwards withdrawn.[7]

A vestigial vestry, now shorn of its secular powers remained. For church purposes, however, it was unsatisfactory since all ratepayers, regardless of their religious beliefs, were potential members of it and the churchwardens, one of whom was usually elected by the parishioners and the other chosen by the vicar, did not need to be Anglicans. Voluntary church councils, therefore, began to make their appearance, encouraged by a bishop or two, and though they had not advanced far when Queen Victoria died, they were to grow into statutory organisations in the twentieth century, charged with the duty to consult with the incumbent on matters of general concern and importance in the parish.

The recreations of his parishioners was a matter to which most incumbents felt it right to devote some attention. It is well known that Keble approved of cricket after Sunday Evensong and initially encouraged it, though he turned against it later because of the opposition that it aroused. An old man in 1874 remembered how as a big boy he had played football on Sunday evenings at Langley Burrell and how the rector tried to stop it by getting hold of the ball and by whipping his knife into the bladder. But another bladder was blown up in a minute and so the rector gave up his attempt in despair. On other days of the week, however, sport could be encouraged. The rector of Livermere in Suffolk was able to open a recreation ground in his parish in the late 1880s, through the kindness of his squire, and thought that cricket, quoits, bowls and rounders tended to bodily good, though he advised the clergy to keep the management of these things in their own hands and to supervise them personally from time to time.[8]

Other activities of the parishioners, however, might give cause for anxiety, and in the country the custom of the parish feast, coming round annually and lasting a week, was especially a time to make a vicar frown. The feast, it seems, was often a week of concentrated immorality and riot, harmless enough in the daytime, but in the evening dangerous to morals since the young men began to haunt the dancing booths set up in the backyards of public houses and beer-shops, where they were soon joined by partners of the other sex, a certain proportion of whom were avowed harlots from the neighbouring town or villages. The remedy, it was suggested, was to give the festival a religious dimension and to preach sermons showing the blessings and evils which resulted from it being well or badly kept. Harvest homes were similarly occasions that needed careful control. Incumbents were advised to start them with a church service, to be followed by a feast in the park, speeches and toasts, and then games— cricket, football, quoits, racing and hurdle jumping. Afterwards a dance round the sheaf was recommended, and then fireworks. 'Don't stint the beer', was the advice given, for it was better to trust in the influence of public opinion, represented by the squire, the clergyman and others, to restrain drunkenness.[9]

In the towns, too, the clergy had problems when they tried to help their parishioners to enjoy themselves. Canon Barnett at Whitechapel, London, arranged for a band to play in a playground on Thursday evenings, but it led to a bacchanalian scene which caused him to stop the band and lock the playground, so bringing down on his head the howls, hoots and stones of the enraged crowd who followed him home.

There were varying opinions on the recreations that the clergy might allow themselves. In the country they were country gentlemen and early in the century engaged naturally and without question in the country pursuits, hunting, shooting and fishing. Ben Newton at Wath kept greyhounds and went coursing, attended the Ripon ball on June 4th, 1817, caught an eel on the twentieth and went partridge shooting in the October of that year. It was a received dogma of ecclesiastical decorum, *The Black Book* announced a few years later, that a parson was not to hunt in a red coat; 'provided only the *Scarlet* does not appear, the revered successor of the apostles may leap over hedge and ditch without the slightest impropriety' it quoted from a letter to the Archbishop of York. At balls, also, the clergy appeared in black, but lavender tints and white might be worn so that it was difficult to distinguish a priest from a layman in a brilliant ballroom, a fact corroborated by Miss Crawford in *Mansfield Park*, who found no distinction of dress between the layman and the clergyman.

But the feeling grew, urged on by the evangelicals and the Tractarians and the greater seriousness in society, that perhaps the clergy should dress in a style different from that of the layman; and that they should not hunt and fish and shoot, nor attend races, balls and theatres. So they began to dress in swallow-tailed coats and white neck-cloths and looked, so their critics said, like waiters. Then the Tractarians and their successors adopted the more distinctive costume of a long, straight coat reaching almost to the heels, something like a cassock, together with a long waistcoat, which was called by the evangelicals the M.B. waistcoat (the Mark of the Beast). This was the outfit of men who were presumed to be on the way to Rome. Later still, the white neck-cloth or tie was abandoned in favour of the dog collar; at Cuddesdon Theological College the last white tie appeared in college photographs in 1883, though the wearing of it never quite died out and it can be found still round the necks of some clergymen. Towards the end of the century some of the younger clergy in the country exchanged the long frock coat for a short black one, pointing out that they needed sometimes to ride bicycles, but the long coat stayed on the backs of clergymen in the towns till after the Queen had died. Black was *de rigeur*, though Mr. Delafield, the new vicar at Candleford Green, was remembered as allowing himself well-worn flannels and a Norfolk jacket in very dark grey for everyday use. Anything lighter would have been too revolutionary. In the summer he appeared in a black-and-white speckled straw boater in place of the round, black, soft felt hat of the other local clergy. In the towns the clergy still wore the tall black hats that went with frock coats.

To these clerical uniforms some of the clergy did not subscribe. Kingsley dressed as a layman except on Sundays. Hawker wore at Morwenstow a claret-coloured coat with long tails, generally open, with a knitted blue fisherman's jersey into which was woven a red cross marking the place where the Lord's side was pierced. He added fishermen's boots reaching to the knee and put on his head in his earlier days a pink or plum beaver hat without a brim, followed by a felt wide-awake one, coloured claret. Dolling at Portsmouth dressed in a well-worn cassock and smoked a cigar, an idiosyncrasy that might be found among advanced anglo-catholics.

The assumption that the clergy should be a race apart manifested itself in little things like the smoking of cigars. 'One must never smoke, without consent, in the presence of a clergyman, and one must never offer a cigar to any ecclesiastic over the rank of a curate,' a book of etiquette advised in 1855. The clergy, then, withdrew from some of the customs and entertainments which their predecessors had enjoyed. Sydney Smith caricatured Blomfield's first instructions to the clergy of the diocese of Chester in well-known, barbed lines which illustrate this process at work:

> Hunt not, fish not, shoot not,
> Dance not, fiddle not, flute not;
> But it is my particular desire
> That once a week you take
> Your dinner with the Squire.

In the middle of the century, it was observed, right-minded men did not like to see a clergyman at a race, a theatre, a ball, a hunting party, a shooting party, a public festival; it was thought unseemly for a clergyman to shoot since it meant putting into the hands of a minister of life, weapons of destruction. Some people did not mind the clergyman fishing, but others did, and when they did the clergyman should give up fishing.[10] Henry Venn Elliott, evangelical minister at Brighton, objected to the theatre and the opera as they were conducted in his day, for opera abounded in such expressions as 'O Dio' and the ballet tolerated an indecent exposure of the person that would be intolerable in a private room or in respectable society. Samuel Wilberforce demanded of his candidates for ordination in 1846, 'Show why indulgence in Field Sports is inconsistent with a devoted Pastoral Ministry,' and he was equally averse to his clergy taking part in cricket matches between the villages. Of course the clergy must avoid drunkenness, scandals over sex, and dishonesty, Walsham

How told divinity students at Cambridge; they should avoid also the lesser dangers of billiards, hunting, fishing, shooting, dancing and card playing.

George Eliot illustrates in *Middlemarch* how the clergy were expected to show restraint in their recreations, for one of the matters that told against Mr. Farebrother, the vicar of St. Botolph's, in the election to the chaplaincy at the Infirmary was the fact that he played, and played for money. There was a billiard-room at the Green Dragon and Mr. Farebrother was a first-rate billiard-player; and though he did not frequent the Green Dragon there were reports that he had been there in the daytime and had won money from his play. He was a good man, chivalrous to his mother, aunt and sister, who depended on him. He filled his church; was sweet-tempered, ready-witted, frank. But in the meeting that chose the chaplain the opinion was voiced that he was too lax for a clergyman and so the appointment went elsewhere.

Yet though the clergy, or some of them, withdrew to some extent from the recreations that their parishioners indulged in, many still took part in these activities. Bishop Christopher Wordsworth discovered a clergyman in his diocese who was breeding and training racehorses and entering them for races under an assumed name. The bishop wrote to him and he resigned his living. Kingsley sat down to dinner one day at four p.m. but when the hunt appeared he was up and off; and in his study there was a fishing-rod, together with reels, feathers and fishing-flies. J. C. Atkinson up at Danby-in-Cleveland, when he wasn't walking, would go fishing and shooting. On December 30th, 1852, the Armstrongs at East Dereham gave a party for forty parishioners, which was to teach them to rejoice when the Church rejoices. It went on till three in the morning and the guests were highly pleased, though a few held back because the society was somewhat mixed. It was difficult to judge rightly the line of demarcation in the society of a country town, Armstrong observed. They were still entertaining nearly thirty years later, when Mrs. Armstrong gave a garden party, which about sixty attended and where the amusements were archery, lawn tennis and pool croquet.

Some of the clergy had no inhibitions about dancing and were even encouraged in it by their superiors. Francis Kilvert dined one night with his vicar and family at the vicarage at six-thirty and went on with them to the ball at Clifford Priory at eight, where fifty-two were present. He danced a quadrille with a young lady who much attracted him and then took her to the cool hall where he found a chair for her screened from general observation by a beautiful azalea. But the young lady's father soon called her and they were obliged to return to the ballroom where he hardly saw her again, except in the gallery when they were drinking claret cup. He got to bed at four thirty just as dawn was breaking. A student preparing for ordination, doubtful whether he should attend a ball during the vacation, wrote to the Principal of his theological college asking for advice and received the singular reply by telegraph, 'Dance, pretty creature, dance.'[11]

For a clergyman was a gentleman and could afford to go to bed as the dawn was breaking, just as the labourers were beginning to stir and to go about a hard day's work. This was generally acknowledged. Dean Gaisford of Christ Church, Oxford, in a sermon told his undergraduates, many of whom would become clergymen, 'Nor can I do better, in conclusion, than impress upon you the study of Greek literature, which not only elevates above the vulgar herd, but leads not infrequently to positions of considerable emolument.' Archdeacon Grantly in *The Last Chronicle of Barset*, published in 1867, meets the Perpetual Curate of Hogglestock and remarks, 'We stand on the only perfect level on which such men can meet each other. We are both gentlemen.'

Towards the end of the century the clergyman's status did begin to decline and bishops and others began to worry about their learning and their breeding. Bishop Ellicott of Gloucester and Bristol noticed it and told a congregation in Bristol Cathedral that there was a silent and most unwelcome decline of learning, and especially of general culture, in the rank and file of the younger clergy. Many had noticed, he said, with some anxiety, a tendency to decline in the social standard and he thought the cause to be the rise of other professions.[12]

Another bishop was heard to say, quite openly, that it was impossible to fathom the depths of ignorance in a candidate for holy orders. Dean Goulburn of Norwich, in his old age in the 1890s, thought that the English clergy, though they were often now more active than their predecessors in the ministry, yet had as a rule sadly deteriorated in that indefinable but yet easily recognised qualification—breeding. Often, he reminisced, in the retired country parsonage had been found the ripe scholar, the profound student, the sound theologian, and they could be the most delightful of entertainers. But alas! they were dying off now, not only because of admission to the ministry of men of a lower social grade, necessitated by the Church's exigencies, but by the pressure, restlessness and breathless hurry of modern life.[13]

But whatever they were like, gentlemen or not gentlemen, and wherever they lived, whether in town or country, the clergy were mortal, like Paul and Barnabas who, when the priest of Jupiter would have honoured them as gods, ran in among the people and told them that they were men with like passions to themselves. Most vicars, most rectors, most clergymen were not cast in the heroic mould of these two saints; but they pointed with wavering fingers to the One whom they believed to be above. When they died, their parishioners mourned them awhile, if they had been good pastors, and then turned to the patrons who would appoint their successors. For life must go on, they knew, and one vicar must follow another; and there would always be a church, it seemed, for there had been a church so long; and the church showed the way to heaven; and the vicar was there to show the way; and perhaps the new vicar would do that better than the old one had done, or perhaps he would not. Who could tell?

NOTES

1 Diana McClatchey, *Oxfordshire Clergy 1777–1869*, p. 194.
2 Hugh McLeod, *Class and Religion in the Late Victorian City*, p. 112.

3 Diana McClatchey, *op. cit.*, pp. 131–2.
4 G. Kitson Clark, *Churchmen and the Condition of England, 1832–1885*, p. 183.
5 John Sandford, *Parochialia*, pp. 341–7.
6 Owen Chadwick, *The Victorian Church*, Pt. II, pp. 155–8.
7 Ibid., p. 199.
8 Herbert James, *The Country Clergyman and his Work*, p. 164.
9 J. H. Blunt, *Directorium Pastorale*, pp. 362–9.
10 R. W. Evans, *The Bishopric of Souls*, pp. 195–7.
11 G. W. E. Russell, *Edward King*, p. 25.
12 C. J. Ellicott, *Some Present Dangers of the Church of England*, p. 34.
13 E. M. Goulburn, *John William Burgon*, Vol. II pp. 361–2.

Bibliography

William ADDISON, *The English Country Parson* (J. M. Dent, 1947).

G. W. O. ADDLESHAW and F. ETCHELLS, *The Architectural Setting of Anglican Worship* (Faber, 1948).

Henry, ALFORD *Life, Journal and Letters*, ed. by his widow (1873).

H. B. J. ARMSTRONG (ed.), *Armstrong's Norfolk Diary* (Hodder and Stoughton, 1963).

A. R. ASHWELL and R. G. WILBERFORCE, *Life of Samuel Wilberforce*, 3 vols. 1880–1883.

J. C. ATKINSON, *Forty Years in a Moorland Parish* (1891).

G. R. BALLEINE, *A History of the Evangelical Party in the Church of England* (1908).

S. BARING-GOULD, *Early Reminiscences 1834–1864* (1923). *The Vicar of Morwenstow* (1899).

Henrietta BARNETT, *Canon Barnett; his Life, work, friends*, 2 vols. (1918).

J. BATEMAN, *Life of Henry Venn Elliott* (1868).

G. BATTISCOMBE, *John Keble ; a study in limitations* (Constable, 1963).

B. A. BAX, *The English Parsonage* (Murray, 1964).

R. BAYNE, (ed.), *Sermons and Lectures* by Brooke Lambert (1902).

G. K. A. BELL, *Randall Davidson, Archbishop of Canterbury*, 2 vols. (Oxford, 1935).

G. F. A. BEST, *Temporal Pillars* (Cambridge, 1964).

Alfred BLOMFIELD, *A Memoir of Charles James Blomfield*, 2nd ed. (1864).

J. H. BLUNT, *Directorium Pastorale* (1864).

J. J. BLUNT, *The Parish Priest*, 5th ed. (1869).

W. BOYD CARPENTER, *Lectures on Preaching* (1895).

H. R. T. BRANDRETH, *Dr. Lee of Lambeth* (S.P.C.K., 1951).

Piers BRENDON, *Hawker of Morwenstow* (Cape, 1975).

C. K. F.BROWN, *A History of the English Clergy 1800–1900* (Faith Press, 1953).

H. J. BURGESS, *Enterprise in Education* (S.P.C.K. 1958).

J. W. BURGON, *A Treatise on the Pastoral Office* (1864). *Lives of Twelve Good Men*, 2 Vols. (1888).

A. J. BUTLER, *Life and Letters of William John Butler* (1898).

S. C. CARPENTER, *Church and People 1789–1889* (S.P.C.K., 1933).

T. T. CARTER, *Richard Temple West* (1895).

W. O. CHADWICK, *The Victorian Church*, 2 Pts. (A. & C. Black, 1966; 1970). *Victorian Miniature* (Hodder and Stoughton, 1960).

J. D. CHAMBERS, and G. E. MINGAY, *The Agricultural Revolution 1750–1880* (Batsford, 1966).

Susan CHITTY, *The Beast and the Monk* (Hodder and Stoughton, 1974).

G. Kitson CLARK, *Churchmen and the Condition of England 1832–1885* (Methuen, 1973). *The Making of Victorian England* (Methuen, 1962).

Basil F. L. CLARKE, *Church Builders of the Nineteenth Century* (S.P.C.K., 1938).

CLERGY LISTS and CROCKFORD'S CLERICAL DIRECTORIES.

CONFIRMATION or THE LAYING ON OF HANDS, by various writers, 2 vols. (S.P.C.K., 1926).

Joyce COOMBS, *George and Mary Sumner* (Sumner Press, 1965).

R. T. DAVIDSON and W. BENHAM, *Life of Archibald*

Campbell Tait Archbishop of Canterbury, 2 vols. (1891).

G. C. B. DAVIES, *Henry Phillpotts* (S.P.C.K., 1954).

H. P. DENISON, *Seventy-two Years' Church Recollections* (1925).

R. W. R. DOLLING, *Ten Years in a Portsmouth Slum* (1896).

John ELLERTON (ed.), *A Manual of Parochial Work* (1888).

E. B. ELLMAN, *Recollections of a Sussex Parson* (1912).

R. W. EVANS, *The Bishopric of Souls*, 5th ed. (1877).

Alice FAIRFAX-LUCY, *Charlecote and the Lucys* (Oxford, 1958).

M. FROST (ed.) *Historical Companion to Hymns Ancient and Modern* (Clowes and Sons, 1962).

Mrs. GASKELL, *The Life of Charlotte Brontë* (Everyman ed., 1970).

Winifred GERIN. *Charlotte Brontë* (Oxford, 1967).

J. C. GILL, *Parson Bull of Byerley*, (S.P.C.K., 1963).

John GOTT, *The Parish Priest of the Town* (1888).

E. M. GOULBURN, *John William Burgon* (1892).

V. H. H. GREEN, *Oxford Common Room* (Arnold, 1957).

R. M. GRIER, *John Allen* (1889).

A. Tindal HART and E. F. CARPENTER, *The Nineteenth Century Country Parson* (Wilding and Son, 1954).

A. Tindal HART, *The Country Priest in English History* (Phoenix House, 1959).

F. D. HOW, *Archbishop Maclagan* (1911). *Bishop Walsham How* (1899).

W. Walsham HOW, *Lectures on Pastoral Work* (1883).

Herbert JAMES, *The Country Clergyman and his Work* (1890).

R. C. D. JASPER, *Prayer Book Revision in England 1800–1900* (S.P.C.K., 1954).

Richard JEFFERIES, *Hodge and His Masters*, 2 vols. (Mac-Gibbon and Kee, 1966).

A. Clifton KELWAY, *George Rundle Prynne* (1905).

KILVERT'S DIARIES, ed. W. Plomer, 2nd ed., 3 vols. (Cape, 1961).

Mary KINGSLEY, *Charles Kingsley. His Letters and Memories of his Life*, 2 vols. (1878).

H. KIRK-SMITH, *William Thomson Archbishop of York* (S.P.C.K., 1958).

G. W. KITCHEN, *E. H. Browne Bishop of Winchester* (1895).

William LAKE, *Memorials of William Charles Lake Dean of Durham*, ed. Katherine Lake (1901).

J. S. LEATHERBARROW, *Victorian Period Piece* (S.P.C.K., 1954).

H. P. LIDDON, *Clerical Life and Work* (1894). *Walter Kerr Hamilton, Bishop of Salisbury* (1869).

J. B. LIGHTFOOT *Ordination Addresses and Counsels to Clergy* (1891).

J. C. LOCKHART, *Cosmo Gordon Lang* (Hodder and Stoughton, 1949).

Norman LONGMATE, *King Cholera* (Hamish Hamilton, 1966).

A. G. LOUGH, *The Influence of John Mason Neale* (S.P.C.K., 1962).

C. F. LOWDER, *Twenty-One Years in St. George's Mission* (1877).

Diana McCLATCHEY, *Oxfordshire Clergy 1777–1869* (Oxford, 1960).

C. C. MACKARNESS, *John Fielder Mackarness, Bishop of Oxford* (1892).

Richard MANT, *The Clergyman's Obligations Considered* (1830). *The Church and Her Ministrations* (1838).

W. L. MATHIESON, *English Church Reform 1815–1840* (1923).

Hugh McLEOD, *Class and Religion in the Late Victorian City* (Croom Helm, 1974).

J. C. MILLER, *Letters to a Young Clergyman* (1878).

W. C. E. NEWBOLT, *Apostles of the Lord* (1901). *The Man of God* (1893). *Speculum Sacerdotum* (1893). *Priestly Ideals*, 2nd ed. (1899). *Priestly Blemishes* (1902).

Benjamin NEWTON, *The Diary of Benjamin Newton, Rector of Wath*, ed. by C. P. Fendall and E. A. Crutchley (Cambridge, 1933).

C. E. OSBORNE, *The Life of Father Dolling* (1903).

William OTTER, *Pastoral Addresses* (1841).

J. H. OVERTON, *The English Church in the Nineteenth Century* (1894).

J. H. OVERTON and Elizabeth WORDSWORTH, *Christopher Wordsworth, Bishop of Lincoln* (1888).

Ashton OXENDEN, *The Pastoral Office* (1857). *The History of My Life* (1891).

Jesse PAGE, *Bishop Patteson* (n.d.).

Eric PARTRIDGE, *Robert Eyres Landor*, (Fanfrolico Press, 1927).

Hesketh PEARSON, *The Smith of Smiths* (Hamish Hamilton, 1934).

M. H. PORT, *Six Hundred New Churches* (S.P.C.K., 1961).

William PURCELL, *Onward, Christian Soldier* (Longmans, 1957).

Michael REYNOLDS, *Martyr of Ritualism. Father Mackonochie of St. Alban's, Holborn* (Faber and Faber, 1965).

F. W. ROBERTSON, *Sermons*, 1st Series, new ed. (1881).

Hugh James ROSE, *The Commission and Consequent Duties of the Clergy* (1828).

G. W. E. RUSSELL, *Edward King, Bishop of Lincoln* (1912).

John SANDFORD, *Parochialia, or Church, School and Parish* (1845).

Alan SAVIDGE, *The Parsonage in England* (S.P.C.K., 1964).

C. H. SIMPKINSON, *Bishop Thorold* (1896).

Archdeacon SINCLAIR, *Thirty-two Years of the Church of England 1842–1874* (1876).

John SKINNER, *Journal of a Somerset Rector, 1803–1834* (Kingsmead, 1971).

B. A. SMITH, *Dean Church* (Oxford, 1958).

Charles SMYTH, *The Art of Preaching* (S.P.C.K., 1953).

W. R. W. STEPHENS, *The Life and Letters of Walter Farquahar Hook,* (1881).

C. J. STRANKS, *Dean Hook* (Mowbrays, 1954).

William STUBBS, *Ordination Addresses* (1901).

H. A. TAINE, *Notes on England* ed. E. Hyams (Thames and Hudson, 1957).

E. S. TALBOT, *The Vocation and Dangers of the Church* (1899).

H. P. THOMAS, *The Church and the Land* (1887).

Flora THOMPSON, *Lark Rise to Candleford*, (Penguin Ed., 1975).

E. D. TOLLEMACHE, *The Tollemaches of Hilmingham and Ham* (W. S. Cowell, 1949).

Henry TWELLS, *Colloquies on Preaching*, 2nd ed. (1889).

John WADE, *The Black Book*, new ed. (1832).

James WHITE, *The Cambridge Movement* (Cambridge, 1962).

E. R. WICKHAM, *Church and People in an Industrial City* (Lutterworth, 1957).

J. R. WOODFORD, *The Great Commission*, 2nd ed. (1887). *Ordination Sermons*, 1872.

Bishops and archdeacons gave numerous Visitation Addresses to their clergy, many of which were printed. These are only occasionally included in the list of books above.

Index